P9-DEY-240

FINGER LICKIN' RIB STICKIN' GREAT TASTIN' HOT & SPICY BARBECUE

By Jane Butel

Illustrations by Jerry Joyner

Workman Publishing, New York

Copyright © 1982 by Jane Butel

All rights reserved.

No portion of this book may be reproduced—
mechanically, electronically, or by any other means,
including photocopying—without written permission of
the publisher. Published simultaneously in Canada by
Saunders of Toronto, Inc.

Library of Congress Cataloging in Publication Data

Butel, Jane.
  Finger lickin', rib stickin', great tastin', hot & spicy
barbecue.

  1. Barbecue cookery. I. Title.
TX840.B3B87   641.5'784 81-43785
ISBN 0-89480-207-0   AACR2
ISBN 0-89480-208-9 (pbk.)

Cover design: Paul Hanson
Cover illustration: Milton Glaser
Book design: Wendy Palitz

Workman Publishing Company, Inc.
1 West 39th Street
New York, N.Y. 10018

Manufactured in the United States of America
First printing August 1982

10 9 8 7 6 5 4

DEDICATION

To all my closest . . . Amy, my daughter,
and my many friends and co-workers, who
really tasted and worked their way through
their weight in ribs so that I could get the
best barbecue tastes, for you to discover!

ACKNOWLEDGMENTS

To dig up, create, and develop this act of
love, I truly thank all who helped,
particularly Kathi Long, my able assistant,
Suzanne Rafer, our always patient and
perfect editor, Kathy Ness, our super
efficient copy editor, and of course Amy, my
daughter, who was always more than
willing to try just one more bite or spoonful
and yield her noble opinion. Together we
have gathered the Rolls Royce recipes for
that goopy bit of heaven we all call
barbecue.

CONTENTS

BARBECUE ANYTIME

Barbecue...Bar-B-Que...Bar-B-Q... Barbeque. The passions generated by this gutsy American dish, no matter how you spell it, are for real although hardly anyone agrees just what barbecue is all about. The answer is far from clear cut and depends on how you define barbecue. To some it means a spicy sauce, to others a cooking style; then there are those who say it's a drippy meat concoction, and to anyone with a backyard it's a festive outdoor party.

Barbecue, as I speak of it in this book, is the saucy stuff with a smoky taste. "Stuff" here means almost any kind of meat; "sauce" means a collection of the best-tasting finger-licking zesty combinations found in this country and given to me by some of America's finest barbecue cooks.

Some originally called for pit-smoked meats but all the recipes have been adapted for home use. And because great barbecue was developed through lots of improvisation, you can continue the tradition—prepare it outdoors on a grill or in a smoker, or indoors on top of the range, in the oven or under the broiler.

PIT SMOKING

The style of cooking meats over an open fire pit has been around since the days of the Peking Man. Many Southern barbecue lovers still consider pit smoking the best method for preparing barbecued meat. There's never been one specific design set up for a pit, but when I was a child you always began with a very large hole about six feet across and four feet deep. Then a layer of heat-resistant rocks was added. A heavy mesh screen was put down over the rocks, then a layer of hardwood such as hickory, oak, alder, or fruit wood. Once the fire got going and the white hardwood coals remained, the prepared meat (the whole, skinned animal) was lowered into the pit on a spit and the pitmasters, as the fire tenders

BBQ LORE
WHAT'S IN A NAME?

There is strong indication that the word "barbecue" comes from the Spanish word *barbacoa* which is derived from an American Indian word for the framework of green wood on which meat or fish was cooked over a pit of coals. Others believe that the French should be credited—when Caribbean pirates came stateside, they roasted animals *barbe-a-queue*, head to tail, so to speak.

were called, used their own carefully guarded secret techniques for getting moist, smoky, succulent results. A good pitmaster was a genius at controlling the low heat for the sixteen hours necessary for the meat drippings to flavor the smoke which, in turn, enriched the smoky taste of the meat.

Nowadays, it's harder to find real outdoor pit barbecue. And pit-cooked no longer necessarily means that the meat had been lovingly tended and basted for hours at a stretch. Also, various states have very stringent laws governing open pits. Consequently many fine barbecue restaurants and all commercial barbecue manufacturers use gas- or electric-fired equipment to control temperatures and conditions. A few landmark restaurants, a number of which are featured in the "Pit Stops" section, use real open pits. And, of course, each of the owners is proud of his or her accomplishment.

Pork shoulders, butts and spareribs are the most popular meats to pit smoke. Once smoked, shoulders and butts are sold "pulled" and partially "pulled." Popularized and most prevalent in the South, "pulled" indicates that the cooked meat has been separated along the grain into shreds with forks or by hand before the sauce is added. Partially "pulled" means that the meat has been partially separated, then cut into one-inch chunks or strands.

Beef is also pit cooked, but requires moister heat than pork. This can be simulated in home methods by tightly covering the cut of meat with a lid or aluminum foil.

SMOKEHOUSE BARBECUING

Smokehouse cooking came along much later than pit smoking and in the U.S. it became popular further north and west. Weather conditions made it a less risky way of smoking meat. It was used to slowly remove moisture from the meat and flavor it at the same time. This procedure was also invaluable for extending the life of the meat. Pork shoulders, butts and ribs are all smoked this way.

Not too many years ago, a smokehouse was simply a large house surrounded with outside pits where hardwood fires were closely watched until the fire burned down to hot coals. The wood chips (presoaked in water overnight) were thrown onto the coals which in turn created a large volume of smoke. The smoke was vented into the smokehouse and smoked the meat.

The meat fat does not drip onto the fire, so smokehouse barbecue tastes different from pit-smoked barbecue. The carbonized charcoal taste is not produced, resulting in a more subtly smoky, drier product which eliminates "pulled" barbecue from the realm of possibility in smokehouse smoking. Each system has its following and most devotees, like myself, love both.

FINGER LICKIN' BARBECUE

Along with great meat preparation, for most of us a successful barbecue ultimately is determined by how delicious the sauce used to marinate, baste, or accompany the meat tastes.

I am convinced that the lack of information on the origins of this saucy American barbecue—spicy, savory and lip-smacking fabulous—stems from the fact that over the years, no one thought of writing down their recipes. Eventually, when recipe-writing developed as a way of sharing formulas for favorite tastes, regional secrets were so jealously guarded that rather than share recipes indiscriminately they were passed on verbally and through demonstration to only the most trusted individuals. This method gave rise, especially in the Southeast and Southwest, to the pitmaster or master barbecuer who was known to exist in most every county during the 1800s.

Each region of the deep South developed definite formulas for barbecue, so today, in some parts of South Carolina and southern Texas, vinegar bastes are used and the sauce is put on after the meat is cooked. In other parts of South Carolina, mustard sauces abound. Further north and east, tomato-base sauces prevail. Sweet, thick, ketchup-base sauces crop up in family formulas throughout the Southwest, some smoky, some not; some hot as fire, others mild. And even to this day in the hardwood forested areas of the Carolinas, Alabama and southeast Texas, good, old-fashioned pits are still used to smoke meats.

You don't need fancy equipment to enjoy barbecue. Although many of the recipes suggest cooking outdoors on a grill, all can be

BBQ LORE

THE BACKYARD BARBECUE

In searching for the origins of barbecue as a backyard event, a story came to my attention in an article written by Orin Anderson entitled "The Quest for the Best Barbecue in the World," published in South Carolina's *Sandlapper* magazine in July 1979. It seems a couple of hundred years ago (or so) a wealthy man named Bernard Quayle decided to throw a get-together for several hundred special friends. Everyone loved it so much that he repeated the event again and again. The food served at these feasts consisted of whole sheep, hogs and steers, roasted over pits. The guests ate this sumptuous feast at long tables set outdoors. Mr. Quayle was not the only rancher to entertain in this fashion, but his parties were so extensive and unusual that the name of his ranch became an expression for pit cooking and outdoor eating: The — (Bar) BQ.

prepared indoors if you have no backyard or if the weather turns ugly. The sauces used for each dish are listed separately in almost every recipe. They can be made in advance and refrigerated or even frozen (see Sauces, page 13). Keep favorites on hand for emergencies—unexpected company, for instance—or to liven up an otherwise dull dish.

Think of barbecue for any season and any time. Remember, you don't need to own a barbecue to throw a barbecue and to serve barbecue!

GETTING STARTED

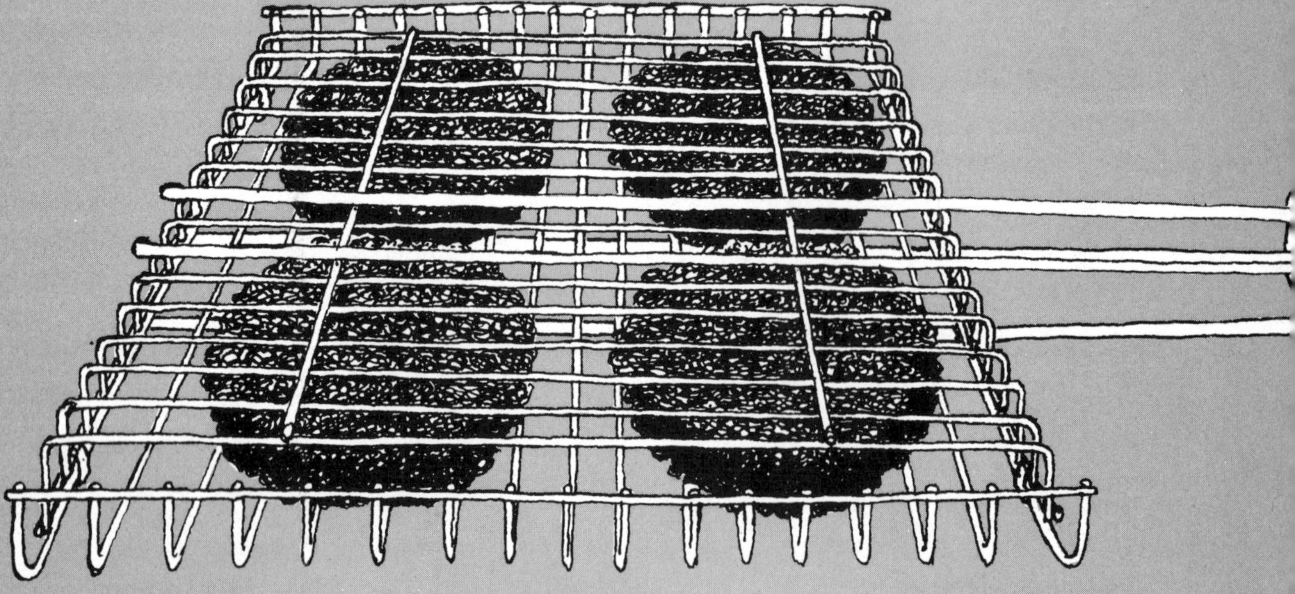

BARBECUE BASICS

Although you may want to go crazy with your newfound barbecue pleasures, don't go hog wild at the beginning. A few simple tools will get you started, and they needn't be expensive. Then you can get more sophisticated equipment if you want, but remember, you can get good barbecue flavor with even the most basic equipment, including your oven broiler. Experimentation is the only real way to master your barbecue technique.

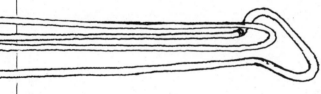

GRILLS

The best bet for the barbecue novice is a small brazier or lightweight folding grill. Both are inexpensive and easy to store.

After that, you may want to purchase a more elaborate model. My choice among these variations would always be a grill with a lid. It will give the food that special smoky flavor—well worth the extra few minutes of cooking time. You can adapt an open brazier grill by making a foil tent, using

heavy-duty broiler foil, to sit over the food as it cooks on the grill and function like a lid. Don't discard your old grill, however, because you can use it for appetizers, breads, and side dishes while the meat cooks on the other one, and you can also store hot coals in it for prolonged cooking on the main grill.

Every type of grill works a little differently. To get the most out of yours, read the manufacturer's instructions thoroughly before using it.

BRAZIER GRILLS The most popular, lightweight, and inexpensive, these range from simple tabletop units to models on wheels with hoods and rotisseries. Larger versions have cranks to adjust the grill height, which aids in controlling cooking temperatures.

HIBACHIS These small, efficient, cast-iron open grills have adjustable grates, air dampers, and coal racks to allow the ashes to fall to the bottom. Perfectly sized for appetizers, small kebobs, and barbecue for two.

KETTLE AND WAGON GRILLS These versatile grills are more expensive. Both types feature lids. Air dampers in the bottom of the grill and in the lid control ventilation and thereby the cooking temperature. When open they function like brazier grills; when closed they work like ovens with the heat controlled by the dampers. You can give the meat a smoked quality by simply adding damp hickory chips to the hot coals and closing the lid.

GAS AND ELECTRIC GRILLS   These grills both work on the radiant-heat principle. Volcanic pumice or ceramic briquettes are placed on racks between the heat source and the grill. Then the heat from the briquettes cooks the food. These grills are extra-convenient versions of the kettle or wagon models; they are easier to start and have more efficient heat control. But for the tastiest results, I prefer cooking over hardwood briquettes to gas or electric grills.

BRIQUETTES

Charcoal briquettes come in two types. Hardwood briquettes are made by burning down oak, hickory, or other hardwoods under controlled heat until they are completely charred. Then they are compressed by a machine into briquettes. Coal briquettes are cheaper but I don't recommend them—you won't get that great smoky taste.

Prepare your charcoal by piling it in a mound in the bottom of the grill, then start your fire. You will need a minimum of 36 briquettes for 3 to 6 pounds of chicken or ribs. If you are barbecuing a roast, add a dozen briquettes for each additional 2 pounds of weight above 3 pounds. After 30 to 45 minutes, when the coals are coated

BBQ HINT

TESTING THE CHARCOAL

One way to test the temperature of the fire is to place the palm of your hand above the coals at the approximate level the food will be cooking:

> 3 inches for beef and lamb
> 4 inches for poultry
> 5 inches for pork

If you can hold your palm steady for:

> 3 seconds, the fire is ready to cook
> 4 seconds, the fire is medium hot (350° F) and you can still start your meat at this temperature
> 5 seconds or more, the fire is too cool to use yet

To raise the temperature, knock the ash from the briquettes and push them closer together. You might also try fanning with a bellows or a folded newspaper. To lower the temperature, distribute the coals farther apart, raise the grill, or mist with water.

with white ash, use a long-handled fork or poker to knock off the ash (which traps the heat inside each briquette).

Spread the coals out evenly in the firebox. It is important to have a spray bottle handy, filled with water for spritzing the coals to produce smoke and to douse flames, as well as long-handled implements and fireproof mitts. By the way, it isn't the flame that cooks the meat, it's the direct infrared radiation from completely heated coals.

Charcoal and wood fires take 30 to 40 minutes to burn down to the ash-covered coals needed for grilling. Outdoor gas cookers take 10 minutes to warm up. Electric grills take approximately 25 minutes.

Position the grill at the proper height for the type of meat you are cooking and place the meat on top. To increase the smokiness, mist the charcoal with the sprayer and close the lid of the grill immediately.

You might also first soak hickory or other hardwood chips in water for 1 hour and add them to the coals when you build your fire, or make the whole fire from hardwood, which will give your meat a subtly smoky taste. Hickory, alder, oak, mesquite, and fruitwoods (orchard trees) are best.

HOME SMOKERS

Once you've tasted some of this great barbecue, you may decide to go even further to get that great down-home taste: a smoker.

Smoking is a slow process. The meat cooks over very low heat in an enclosed space, smoke and moisture circulating around it to create that special succulence. With such a slow, gentle method, meat shrinks very little.

Smoking may or may not totally cook the meat, so you should make sure that whatever you are smoking reaches a safe internal temperature (pork especially). Generally you can smoke the meat long enough so that it needs no additional cooking in an oven. But if you are in doubt, a little extra heating won't hurt.

GAS OR ELECTRIC SMOKERS These are simple box-like structures with a heating element in the bottom, a pan that fits on top of the heat and holds the smoldering chips or chunks of wood, and racks located above these to hold the item being smoked. They are thermostatically controlled, and are mini-versions of the kind of smokers used in barbecue restaurants.

If you buy a small electric smoker, save the box. It turns out to be the key to the whole smoking operation, especially in cold weather. The cardboard packing box should be left around the smoker when it is in use, acting as an insulator to keep the heat in.

CHARCOAL OR WOOD SMOKERS These smokers are rather small and look like a loaf cake pan

The barrel smoker is a barbecue apparatus made from a surplus steel drum, mounted on its side to a metal stand.

sitting double-deck over another loaf cake pan. They are used the world around relying on hardwood chips, coals or sawdust for their smoke. The advantage of these cookers is their simplicity. Their disadvantage is that they require careful watching. A smoky fire must be maintained and the heat, approximately 180°F, depending on the cut and type of meat you are smoking, must be kept even.

CHARCOAL WATER SMOKERS AND CHINESE SMOKERS The water smoker functions much like standard charcoal smokers, with the addition of a pan of liquid (water and marinade) placed between the charcoal and the grill, so that the meat in effect self-bastes during the smoking process, adding to its juiciness. (They also come in electric versions.)

Chinese smokers, whether permanent brick or movable metal, are always L-shaped, with an upright chimney. The meat hangs from hooks in the chimney, away from the coals, and the food is cooked in the hot smoke.

DO-IT-YOURSELF EQUIPMENT I've seen dozens of ingenious homemade smokers—using mailboxes, garbage cans, refrigerators—many of them as efficient as store-bought ones. They all work on the basic principles: heating element in the bottom (an old hot plate, for instance), something to hold the wood chips (a cast-iron frying pan), a rack for the food (a discarded canning rack, perhaps), and ventilation. There's no stopping the determined smoking enthusiast!

WOOD

Storebought smokers come supplied with a starter package of wood chips, If you use larger chunks of wood you won't need to check the smoker as frequently. Or you can use a mixture of the chips and larger chunks of wood. A combination of one-third each of packaged chips, chunks and water works quite well. And, I might add, a little wood goes a long way. The wood should be soaked in water, kept wet, and replenished throughout the smoking process.

Use only hardwoods. Softwoods such as pine are not used for smoking because the resins give the meat an unpleasant taste. I found that hickory works best for beef and pork and that apple wood gives poultry a wonderful flavor. You can usually purchase wood chips and chunks from the makers of the smokers.

TOOLS

Here, too, a few essential items do the trick. Some of them are just long-handled versions of familiar kitchen implements designed to keep you away from the hot coals.

TONGS: two pairs with long handles, one for food and one for coals. (Always turn meat with tongs to avoid puncturing it and losing precious juices.)

METAL SPATULA: long-handled, for turning food.

FORK: long-handled, for prodding and pulling vegetables, never meat.

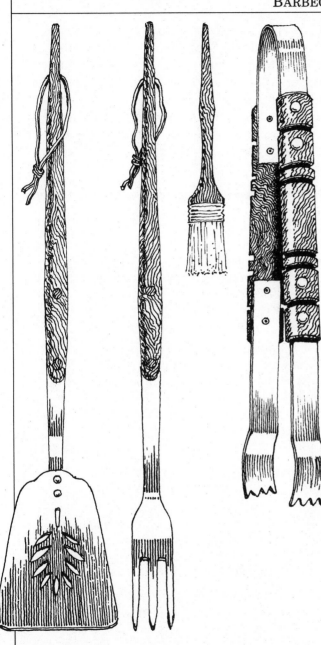

BASTING BRUSH: long-handled, for brushing sauce onto the meat during the cooking process.

HINGED WIRE GRILL BASKET: for foods that require frequent turning such as burgers, chops and shrimp.

ASBESTOS GLOVES OR MITTS: for adjusting the rack, turning the basket.

MEAT THERMOMETER: for larger cuts, because from the way it looks on the outside, you may think the meat is done when it isn't.

PLANT MISTER OR PUMP SPRAY BOTTLE FILLED WITH WATER: to douse flare-ups.

SAUCES

Sauces add considerably to the difference in flavor from one barbecue to another. Each part of the country has its own favorite, and I've tested and tasted for years to determine the very best of these.

Sauces vary: There are sweet ketchup-base Middle South ones; tart mustard or vinegar types from the Carolinas; garlicky, spicy-hot Southwestern versions; plus fruity ones and Orient-inspired soy-ginger-garlic sauces from the West Coast. And of course there are shades of everything else in between.

Personally, I've always preferred thick, red, strongly spiced, sweet-sour, smoky, garlicky sauces with a pungent flavor balance, using the freshest and purest ingredients.

Whatever your preference, the sauces here are the *best* of what it takes from all over the U.S. to make home-cooked, finger-lickin' barbecue.

These sauces can be used over meats, poultry and fish cooked in your oven broiler or outdoors on the grill. I usually choose indoor barbecuing for the sauces with a high sugar content since the sauce tends to blacken less when cooked indoors.

I've suggested my favorite pairings of sauces and meats or fish—but don't limit yourself. Try your own favorites on something different and you'll discover even more gorgeous combinations! (They can be used when you're smoking meats, too. Follow the manufacturer's instructions for smoking—then add the sauce and dig in.) Barbecue

SAUCE NOTES

Most of the recipes that follow make enough sauce for you to have extra at the table—and also leave you some to freeze. I've listed the maximum amount of meat the sauce will cover, but of course you can cook less and save the additional sauce for another meal.

★ Allow ⅓ to ½ cup of sauce per pound of meat.

★ Leave the pot uncovered when you're cooking the sauce so it will reduce to its desired consistency.

★ The amount of salt given in the recipes is only a guide. You may want to wait and add salt to taste after the sauce has finished cooking—a great many sauce ingredients contain substantial amounts of salt and when reduced become even saltier.

★ As a rule, do not start basting meat with a ketchup- or tomato-base sauce until the meat is one-third done, as the sugar and sweeteners in the ingredients have a tendency to burn quickly over high heat.

★ All sauces can be prepared ahead and stored in the refrigerator for up to a week—or keep them in the freezer for as long as three months. They'll make an ordinary meat dish special.

★ To eliminate loss of sauce, prevent sauce from burning, and to facilitate cleanup, cover the grill with heavy-duty aluminum foil and punch holes in the foil with a knife to allow for ventilation. But sear the meat first on both sides before placing it on the foil. This will seal in the smoky taste.

★ Serve leftover sauce along with the cooked meat.

★ When storing in the refrigerator, do not use foil to cover meats cooked with an acid-base sauce (tomato or lemon, for example) because the sauce will eat holes in the foil, which will taint the flavor of the sauce and the meat.

★ If you marinated meat in the sauce, wipe the sauce off with a paper towel before searing the meat, so it will brown well.

sauce improves nearly every edible it gets put on, and that includes potato chips or fries, and all sorts of vegetables whether steamed, roasted, or served raw as crudités.

MARINADE

A marinade is an aromatic blend of herbs and vegetables in which meat, poultry or fish can be soaked so it will absorb the flavors and become more tender. Usually the ingredients include oil to lubricate the flesh and an additional liquid, most often an acid (wine, vinegar, or fruit juice), which serves to tenderize the meat. A baste, on the other hand, is a liquid which is applied to the food as it cooks, giving a flavor to the surface.

Barbecue sauces ordinarily are brushed onto the food as it cooks, as a baste. However, since they contain many of the same ingredients, they can function as a marinade also.

For small cuts allow 1 hour per inch of thickness, at room temperature; and 3 hours per inch of thickness when refrigerated. For larger cuts of meat allow 4 to 6 hours at room temperature, or from 1 to 2 days in the refrigerator, depending on the size of the cut. Turn the meat occasionally to distribute the marinade. Just remember to wipe off any extra sauce before you sear the meat in order for it to brown well.

Always marinate in a noncorrosive container such as glass, porcelain, glazed earthenware or stainless steel. Leave the dish uncovered to allow air to circulate.

BBQ HINT

COOKING MEATS

★ If meat is to be cooked without sauce, oil the grill with 1 to 2 tablespoons of vegetable or olive oil to prevent the meat from sticking to it. Or, you may grease it with the fat trimmed from the meat to be cooked.

★ Cook pork slowly and thoroughly: for fresh pork, 20 to 25 minutes per inch of thickness; for smoked pork, 15 to 20 minutes per inch of thickness.

★ Meat will cook faster if brought to room temperature (70°F) in advance. This takes about 20 to 30 minutes in a warm kitchen and up to 1 hour in a cooler room, depending on the cut and size of the meat.

★ Trim cuts of meat of all excess fat before grilling, leaving ¼ inch around the edges.

★ Cuts of beef and lamb for outdoor grilling should be a minimum of 1½ inches thick, but not more than 3 inches thick, to remain pink inside after the surface sears. Pork should always be at least 1 inch thick, but never thicker than 1½ inches because thorough cooking is necessary.

★ Ribs will be juicier if they are cooked in large pieces (racks). If cut into serving pieces, they'll be crisp and more surfaces will be glazed with the sauce. In true barbecue, the meat is never touched by the flame.

LIQUID SMOKE

Basically, the easiest way to gain a smoky taste in any barbecue or curing process is to carefully apply liquid smoke. Made by burning damp hickory wood, condensing the smoke and scientifically processing it to remove the tars and resins, the U.S. Department of Agriculture considers liquid smoke a natural food product. It contains no calories and has been accepted as a "legal" product for dieters. It contains less than 1 milligram of sodium per tablespoon.

ROASTING TEMPERATURES

(Place meat thermometer in the center, not touching the bone.)

BEEF	Rare - 140° F
	Medium - 160° F
	Well done - 170° F
PORK	170° F
CHICKEN	Breast - 170° F
	Thigh - 180° F
DUCK	Thigh - 170° F
TURKEY	Breast - 170° F
	Thigh - 180° F
LAMB	Rare - 140° F
	Medium - 160° F
	Well done - 170°–180° F

Liquid smoke seems to have originated in Kansas City and was first marketed, in 1895, in Ulysses, Nebraska, by one family, the Wrights. It was an immediate success because it replaced time-consuming smokehouse techniques with an easy-to-use liquid. Once the meat was cured, the smoky taste could be brushed on or added drop by drop, saving much energy.

Wright's Liquid Smoke is still in business and has relocated to Tennessee. The bottles are much fancier nowadays; they've even come up with a spray bottle so that you don't have to pour it onto the meat. When I was a kid, you had to let the liquid smoke drip very carefully. We always used a soft cloth to dab it sparingly on the meat, and even then only used it when time and circumstance prevented enjoying and taking part in the real thing.

Using this product is really a matter of personal preference. It works well and tastes great when used in the proper proportions. Because of its concentrated nature, liquid smoke should be added with discretion to sauces. I still feel that nothing really substitutes for the real smoke.

For source information see the mail-order section.

LET'S BARBECUE

OUTDOOR BARBECUE

Barbecuing on your outdoor grill, when you follow these recipes, results in finger lickin', sumptuously sauced meats, not just simple steaks or chops! These very finest of sauce recipes from all over the U.S.A., coupled with hearty ribs and chops, chicken and seafood, should tempt you to dust off your grill and allow yourself to experience the passionate delights of authentic, honest-to-goodness, old-fashioned barbecue.

JANE'S BEST BARBECUED RIBS

This sauce has developed over the years, until now it's a real winner and my all-time Southwestern favorite. It is particularly great served over lean baby back pork ribs, but you can also serve it on chicken. Ears of corn grilled in the husk, freshly baked cornbread and homemade coleslaw served alongside make a fabulous feast.

2 tablespoons bacon drippings

1 medium Spanish onion, finely chopped

1 clove garlic, minced

14-ounce bottle ketchup

6 tablespoons Worcestershire sauce

2 tablespoons cider vinegar

¼ cup dry white wine

1 teaspoon dry mustard

2 tablespoons dark brown sugar, packed

1 to 2 tablespoons pure ground hot red chile, or to taste

1 to 2 tablespoons pure ground mild red chile, or to taste

¼ teaspoon cayenne pepper or pequin quebrado (this is preferable, if you can get it)

¾ teaspoon ground cumin

¼ teaspoon ground coriander seed

1 teaspoon liquid smoke

4 to 6 pounds baby back pork ribs, in uncut racks

TO PREPARE THE SAUCE

1. Melt the bacon drippings in a 2-quart saucepan over medium heat, then add the onion and garlic, and sauté until the onion is transparent.

2. Add the remaining ingredients through the liquid smoke, reduce the heat to low, and simmer, uncovered, for 15 minutes, stirring occasionally. Set the sauce aside until you are ready to use it.

TO BARBECUE THE RIBS

1. When the fire is ready, position the rack 3 inches above the heat source. Place the racks of ribs on the grill and sear the meat for 2 minutes per side.

2. Remove the meat from the grill, raise the rack 2 inches, and cover it with a layer of heavy-duty broiler foil. Puncture the foil to make plenty of ventilation holes.

3. Place the ribs on the foil and generously spoon on the barbecue sauce. Allow the ribs to cook for 15 minutes before turning them and saucing the second side.

4. Once the second side is basted, cook the ribs for an additional 15 minutes before turning and saucing them again.

5. Allow the ribs to grill for 10 minutes, then turn and sauce them one final time. After 10 more minutes both sides of the ribs should have a crisp glaze. Continue saucing and turning until a sharp knife inserted between the ribs shows no pink meat.

6. Transfer the racks to a carving board, cut the ribs apart and pile them on platters for guests to help themselves.

Yield: 3 cups sauce
Serves: 4 to 6

JAMES BEAL'S BARBECUED RIBS

In the spring of 1981, John Hinterberger of the Seattle *Times* discovered that town's J.K. Wild Boar Soul BBQ Pit and its affable owner, James Beal, a Dallas native. In his laudatory review of Beal's great barbecue, Hinterberger says that according to Beal, what really makes barbecue work is long, slow cooking, preferably in a smoke chamber indirectly heated by the fire source. (The ribs at the Wild Boar cook a minimum of 14 hours at very low temperatures. Folks have been known to faint with anticipation.)

Beal seasons the meat only slightly during cooking, dusting it with a mixture of seasoned salt and paprika. The barbecue sauce goes on afterward; otherwise, the sugar would turn the ribs black during the cooking process. The meat receives its final glaze of gorgeous goop when it is served. You need to spend as much time fussing with it as you do with the meat.

¾ *cup granulated sugar*

½ *cup dark brown sugar, packed*

⅔ *cup rich, dark beef base made from double-strength beef bouillon or consommé*

1 quart hot water

⅔ *cup prepared mustard (ball-park variety)*

⅓ *cup white vinegar*

⅓ *cup liquid smoke*

⅔ *cup Worcestershire sauce*

1⅓ cups tomato paste (10⅔ ounces)

3 tablespoons pure ground hot red chile, or to taste

5 medium-size marinated jalapeño peppers, finely diced

12 pounds baby back ribs, in uncut racks

2 teaspoons seasoned salt

2 teaspoons paprika

To Prepare the Sauce

1. In a 3-quart saucepan, mix the sugars and the beef base in the water. Cook over medium heat until the mixture is dissolved.

2. Add the remaining ingredients through the jalapeños and simmer, uncovered, over low heat for 2 hours. Set aside until you are ready to barbecue.

To Barbecue the Ribs

1. When the fire is ready, position the rack 3 inches above the heat source. Sprinkle the ribs on both sides with the seasoned salt and the paprika. Place the racks of ribs on the grill and sear the meat for 2 minutes per side.

2. When the meat is seared, raise the rack 2 inches. Allow the ribs to cook for 15 minutes before turning them.

3. Once the second side has cooked turn the ribs and cook them for an additional 15 minutes before turning them again.

4. Allow the ribs to grill for 10 minutes more, then turn them one final time. After another 10 minutes both sides of the ribs should have a crisp glaze. The ribs will be done when a sharp knife inserted between the ribs shows no pink meat.

5. Transfer the racks to a carving board, cut the ribs apart and pile them on platters for guests to serve themselves, accompanied, of course, by some of James Beal's fabulous sauce.

Yield: 1½ quarts sauce
Serves: 10 to 12

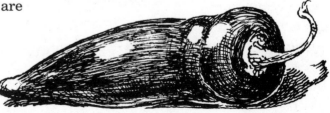

SUPER SECRET BABY BACK PORK RIBS

A retired cook shared this secret with me, because I promised not to reveal the name of the restaurant that made these ribs famous. When created in their original setting the ribs were specially smoked, but this backyard version is just as irresistibly delicious. Serve them with crusty hollows of sourdough garlic bread (see Note).

1 tablespoon Worcestershire sauce
½ cup cider vinegar
2 cups tomato sauce
½ cup dark brown sugar, packed
1 large clove garlic, finely minced
¼ teaspoon celery salt
Pinch of allspice

1 tablespoon freshly grated onion
2 tablespoons pure ground hot red chile
¼ teaspoon cayenne pepper or pequin quebrado (this is preferable, if you can get it)
4 pounds baby back pork ribs, in uncut racks

To Prepare the Sauce

In a 2-quart saucepan, combine the ingredients through the cayenne pepper and simmer, uncovered, over low heat until the sauce is thickened. Set the sauce aside until you are ready to use it.

To Barbecue the Ribs

1. This barbecue sauce also works well as a marinade. About 2 to 4 hours before you are planning to cook the meat, place the racks of ribs in a roasting pan large enough to hold them in a single layer. You may need to divide the meat between two pans. To marinate use only ½ to ⅔ of the sauce and spoon it over the meat, making sure both sides are well covered. Of the remaining sauce, reserve half to serve with the cooked ribs. Reserve the rest to use as a baste during the cooking.

2. Let the marinating ribs sit, uncovered, and turn after each hour. Spoon sauce over the racks after each turn. Do not refrigerate the ribs during the marinating time as refrigeration slows down the meat's ability to absorb flavors.

3. When you are ready to cook the meat, remove the ribs from the marinade. Add the marinade to the sauce you reserved.

4. Position the grill rack 3 inches above the heat source. Place the racks of ribs on the grill and sear the meat for 5 minutes per side.

5. Remove the meat from the grill, raise the rack another 2 inches, and cover it with a layer of heavy-duty broiler foil. Puncture the foil to make ventilation holes.

6. Place the ribs on the foil and generously spoon on the reserved basting sauce. Allow the ribs to cook for 15 minutes before turning them and saucing the second side.

7. Once the second side is basted, cook the ribs for an additional 15 minutes before turning and saucing again.

8. Allow the ribs to grill for 10 minutes then turn and sauce them one final time. After 10 more minutes both sides of the ribs should have a crisp glaze.

9. Transfer the racks to a carving board, cut the ribs apart into easy-to-serve portions and pile them on platters for guests to help themselves. Serve with the sauce specifically reserved for table use.

Yield: 3 cups sauce
Serves: 4

Note: For an average, foot-long loaf of garlic bread: In a small saucepan melt 4 tablespoons unsalted butter with ¼ cup olive oil over low heat, then add freshly minced garlic to taste. Raise the heat and brown the garlic for a few seconds. Halve the bread lengthwise, brush the butter and garlic mixture on each half and toast them in the oven or over the grill.

FIERY HOT AND SOUTH CAROLINA PORK

These recipes come from David Brown, owner of the famous Hickory House Pit BBQ in Winnsboro, South Carolina. He has a strong preference for these sauces because they don't hide the pork flavor as ketchup- or mustard-base sauces have a tendency to do. Both sauces are too strong to be used as a marinade and neither needs to be cooked before using it to baste the pork. The meat should be cooked in a kettle or wagon type of grill (see page 9), and the cooking instructions that follow are good for both sauce recipes.

FIERY HOT BASTING SAUCE

2 cups cider vinegar
1 tablespoon Worcestershire sauce
1 tablespoon finely ground black pepper
1 tablespoon liquid hot pepper sauce
½ tablespoon salt, or to taste
2 pounds pork butt or shoulder

In a bowl, combine all the ingredients and mix well. Allow the flavors to mellow for at least 1 hour at room temperature.

Yield: 2 cups sauce
Serves: 4

SOUTH CAROLINA BASTING SAUCE

2 cups cider vinegar
1 tablespoon finely ground black pepper
1 tablespoon cayenne pepper
1 tablespoon vegetable oil
2 pounds pork butt or shoulder

Combine all the ingredients in a bowl and mix well. Allow the flavors to mellow for at least 1 hour at room temperature.

Yield: 2 cups sauce
Serves: 4

TO BARBECUE THE PORK

(for either sauce recipe)

1. When the fire is ready, position the rack 5 inches above the heat source. Place the meat on the grill and sear it for 2 minutes per side.

2. When the meat is seared, baste it and close the lid on the grill.

3. After 15 minutes turn the meat and baste again, then close the lid. Continue turning and basting every 15 minutes until the meat falls from the bone, about 1- to 1½-hours.

4. Transfer the meat to a cutting board, cut it into bite-size pieces and serve.

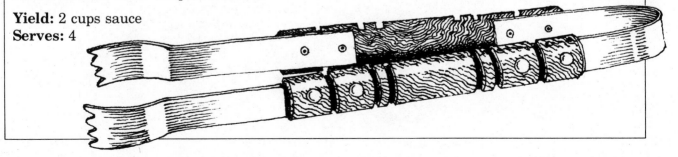

"BBC's" (BEER BARBECUED PORK CHOPS)

Bill Zubke, 1979 winner of the South Dakota Pork Cookout, developed this winning recipe using a well-seasoned brew which he serves on pork loin chops.

¼ cup cider vinegar

¼ cup Worcestershire sauce

¼ cup unsalted butter

1 medium onion, chopped

1 tablespoon celery seed

2 cloves fresh garlic, finely minced

1 teaspoon dry mustard

1 teaspoon granulated sugar

1 teaspoon salt

1 teaspoon pepper, either cayenne or freshly ground black

14-ounce bottle ketchup

1 cup flat beer (fresh beer will work, too)

8 loin pork chops, 1- to 1¼-inches thick

TO PREPARE THE SAUCE

In a 2-quart saucepan, combine all the ingredients through the beer. Simmer, uncovered, over medium heat for 15 minutes. Stir frequently to blend the flavors. Set the sauce aside until you are ready to barbecue.

TO BARBECUE THE CHOPS

1. When the fire is ready, position the rack 3 inches above the heat source. Place the chops on the rack and sear the meat for 5 minutes on each side.

2. Remove the chops from the grill. Raise the rack another 2 inches, and cover it with a layer of heavy-duty broiler foil. Poke ventilation holes in the foil.

3. Return the chops to the grill and generously spoon on the sauce. Cook for 10 minutes, then turn the meat and generously sauce the second side.

4. Continue turning and saucing the chops every 5 minutes until they are cooked through, a total of 30 to 40 minutes. To test for doneness, cut through to the bone of a chop. If the meat is white, with no pink showing, the chop is done.

Yield: 3 cups sauce
Serves: 4

HAMBURGERS MADE SPECIAL

Use leftover barbecue sauce to make hamburgers something special. Don't add the sauce to the raw meat. First sear the burger on one side, then turn it and sauce the cooked side. When the second side is seared, turn the burger again and sauce the second side. Continue to cook and sauce the hamburger until it's done to your taste.

These taste especially good on burgers:
★ Jane's Best (page 20)
★ James Beal's (page 22)
★ Super Secret (page 24)
★ Outrageous (page 43)
★ Down Home Louisiana (page 44)
★ Jerry's Beef (page 58)
★ San Francisco (page 68)

New Mexico Barbecued Beef Ribs

Short ribs, straight from the hills of Sante Fe, New Mexico. Served northern New Mexico style, they would be accompanied by stewed pinto beans, more of the red chile sauce, green chile relish (see Note), and steaming homemade wheat tortillas. A simple vegetable salad and lots of cold Mexican beer followed by Mexican coffee, tart, chilled fresh fruits and crisp, sweet, spicy cookies (New Mexican anise-flavored biscochitos, if possible) for dessert complete this feast with minimal work.

⅓ cup Red Chile Sauce (recipe follows)
1 cup dry red wine
2 tablespoons olive oil
1 large clove garlic, minced
1 small Spanish onion, diced
½ teaspoon salt
¼ teaspoon freshly ground black pepper
4 pounds beef short ribs

To Prepare the Sauce

1. The night before your barbecue, prepare the Red Chile Sauce.

2. Two hours before your barbecue, combine all the ingredients including the ⅓ cup Red Chile Sauce, but not the ribs, in a mixing bowl. Allow the marinade to sit at room temperature for 15 minutes to blend flavors.

TO BARBECUE THE RIBS

1. Spread the ribs out in a roasting pan, large enough to hold them in a single layer. Pour the sauce over the ribs, making sure each one is well covered. Turn and rub the ribs with sauce several times. It is not necessary to refrigerate the ribs.

2. When the fire is ready, position the rack 3 inches above the heat source. Remove the ribs from the marinade and reserve the marinade in a bowl or pitcher.

3. Place the ribs on the grill and sear for 10 minutes each side.

4. Remove the ribs from the grill, raise the rack another 2 inches above the heat source, and cover it with a layer of heavy-duty broiler foil. Poke ventilation holes in the foil. Return the ribs to the grill and spoon on the reserved marinade. Cook for 5 minutes, then turn and baste the second side.

5. Continue turning and basting every 5 minutes until the ribs are done, 30 to 40 minutes. The meat should be slightly pink inside and crusty brown outside.

Note: Prepare green chile relish by roasting green chiles alongside the ribs until charred. While the meat continues to cook, quickly chill (a freezer will do it quickly), peel, and dice the chiles. Add freshly minced garlic and salt, and your relish is ready.

Yield: 1⅔ cups sauce
Serves: 4

BBQ DIP

RED CHILE SAUCE

You will need only ⅓ cup of this sauce for the barbecue marinade. The additional sauce should be served at the table.

2 tablespoons bacon drippings or lard
2 tablespoons flour
¼ cup pure ground mild red chile, or to taste
2 cups beef bouillon or water
1 clove garlic, finely minced
¾ teaspoon salt, or to taste
¼ teaspoon ground oregano (Mexican, if you can get it)
¼ teaspoon ground cumin

1. In a 2-quart saucepan, melt the drippings or lard over medium heat. Slowly add the flour, stirring to combine thoroughly, and cook the mixture until it turns golden.

2. Remove the pan from the heat and stir in the chile. When it is well-incorporated add the bouillon, stir, and return the pan to the heat.

3. Add the remaining ingredients and simmer, uncovered, for 30 minutes or longer to develop the flavor.

4. Taste, and adjust the seasonings if necessary. Allow the sauce to cool, then transfer it to an airtight container and refrigerate.

Yield: 2 cups sauce

TERRY JOHNSON'S HAWAIIAN LUAU BARBECUED BEEF RIBS

Hailing from Hawaii and winner of the Nevada State Chili Contest in 1980, Terry has another passion...barbecue! She uses this marinade with meaty beef short ribs and the raves don't stop. Serve them Hawaiian style surrounded by flowers and orange wedges or by pineapple slices. Accompany the ribs with rice molds (see Note). A fresh fruit salad tops off this perfect barbecue.

1 cup soy sauce

6 tablespoons dark brown sugar, packed

1 cup water

⅔ cup dry sherry

2 teaspoons pure ground hot red chile, or to taste

2 teaspoons Chinese Five Spice powder*

3 teaspoons minced fresh ginger

2 teaspoons minced garlic

4 to 6 pounds beef short ribs

TO PREPARE THE SAUCE

In a small saucepan combine all the ingredients through the garlic. Cook over medium heat to dissolve the sugar, but do *not* boil. Remove the marinade from the heat and let it cool. Set it aside until you are ready to marinate the ribs.

To Barbecue the Ribs

1. Two hours before your barbecue, spread the ribs out in a roasting pan, large enough to hold them in a single layer. You may need to divide the meat between two pans. Pour the sauce over the ribs, making sure all the meat is well covered. Turn and rub the ribs with sauce several times during the marinating period. It is not necessary to refrigerate the ribs.

2. When the fire is ready, position the rack 3 inches above the heat source.

3. Remove the ribs from the marinade and reserve the marinade in a bowl or pitcher, including any excess scraped off the ribs.

4. Place the ribs on the grill and sear for 10 minutes each side.

5. Spoon on the reserved marinade a little at a time after each turn. Cook for 5 minutes, then turn and baste the second side.

6. Continue turning and basting every 5 minutes until the ribs are done, 30 to 40 minutes. The meat should be slightly pink on the inside and crusty brown on the outside.

Yield: 2⅔ cups sauce
Serves: 4 to 6

*Chinese Five Spice powder is available at Chinese specialty stores and in the gourmet food section of some supermarkets.

Note: Make rice molds by simply pressing cooked rice into ⅓-cup-size buttered ramekins, then steaming them in an inch of water for about 10 minutes before unmolding and serving. You could also add some of the marinade to the unmolded cooked rice plus 2 tablespoons each of chopped Bermuda onion and slivered toasted almonds. Garnish each portion of rice with minced parsley after you unmold it.

ALABAMA SMOKY BARBECUED CHICKEN

This recipe (dedicated to Harold Newman of Waverly, Alabama) comes to me courtesy of Pfaffman Studios, Brooklyn, New York, where my friends Scott Pfaffman and Florence Neil have the most fabulous outdoor barbecues on the roof of their loft. Their chicken is cooked in homemade barrel smokers but you can get the same effect with any covered grill. It's some of the best barbecued chicken I've come across in quite a while.

4 cups tomato sauce
½ cup light soy sauce
½ cup white vinegar
12 ounces flat beer (fresh beer will work, too)
1 tablespoon salt
1 tablespoon pure ground hot red chile
1 tablespoon freshly ground black pepper
3 large cloves garlic, finely minced
8 3- to 4-pound chickens, quartered or cut
   into serving pieces

1. Preheat the oven to 450° F.

2. In a 2-quart saucepan combine all ingredients through the garlic and allow the sauce to simmer, uncovered, over low heat for 20 minutes. Stir to combine well.

3. Meanwhile, place the chicken pieces in large oiled baking pans skin side up and bake for 45 minutes in the preheated oven.

4. Remove the chicken from the oven. Pour off the collected pan juices and fat, reserving 1 cup. Add this cup to the sauce ingredients on the stove.

5. Bring the sauce to a boil, then lower the heat and simmer for 15 minutes.

6. Pour the sauce over the chicken (still in the pans) and marinate the chicken in it for 1 hour at room temperature, basting frequently with the sauce.

7. In the meantime, start the fire in your grill, using wood scraps (not charcoal lighter). When the fire is ready, cover the rack with a layer of heavy-duty broiler foil (puncture it with plenty of holes for ventilation) and position it 5 inches above the heat source. Remove the chicken from the marinade. Pour the marinade into a bowl to use to baste the chicken as it grills. Place the chicken on the rack, skin side up, and cover the grill with its lid (or with a foil tent; puncture plenty of holes for ventilation). You want the chicken to cook slowly.

8. Baste the chicken with the sauce frequently, then turn the pieces after 30 minutes. Keep the fire under control by occa-

sionally spraying it with water from a spray bottle. Continue cooking the chicken, basting often, for 60 to 70 minutes, or until it is very tender and smoky.

9. When the chicken is cooked, remove it from the grill and serve it with the remaining sauce.

Serves: 12 to 15

TO MAKE A FOIL TENT
(for a grill with no cover)

To create this pyramid-shape lid for your grill you need two 4- by 4-foot lengths of 18-inch-wide, heavy-duty broiler foil.

Lay one sheet of foil on top of the other, dull side out. Fold together one long edge, making first a ¼-inch fold, then a second ¼-inch fold. Open up the foil. You should have one big sheet securely fastened down the center.

Halfway along each long and short side, make a deep tuck. The foil should peak in the center to make a pyramid-shape tent, shiny side in. To stabilize the tent, turn up an inch all along the bottom edge.

Place the tent over your grill after the meat has been placed on the rack. Using the tent will add to the smoky flavor of the meat.

SUNNY ARIZONA'S SPECIAL CHICKEN

This spicy-hot sauce also tastes wonderful when added to a "pulled" pork butt. For instructions on how to "pull" meat see page 55.

4 pickled jalapeño peppers, stemmed, seeded and finely minced

2 large cloves garlic, finely minced

1 teaspoon dry mustard

1 teaspoon each dried sweet basil and oregano, rubbed to a powder

2 teaspoons kosher salt (coarse) salt

3 tablespoons fresh orange juice

¼ cup honey

3 tablespoons red wine vinegar

2 tablespoons vegetable oil

1 small onion, finely minced

3 cups crushed canned tomatoes

5 to 6 pounds chicken, cut into serving pieces

TO PREPARE THE SAUCE

1. Make sure the jalapeños and garlic are very finely minced.

2. In a ceramic bowl, combine the minced peppers and garlic with the dry mustard, basil, oregano, salt, orange juice, honey, and vinegar. Set aside.

3. In a 2-quart saucepan, heat the oil over medium heat, then add the onion and sauté until softened but not browned. Stir in the tomatoes and add the mixture set aside in Step 2.

4. Bring the sauce to a boil. Reduce the heat and simmer, uncovered, stirring occasionally, for 40 minutes, or until it has been reduced to a desirable thickness.

5. Taste and correct the seasonings.

TO BARBECUE THE CHICKEN

1. When the fire is ready, position the rack 5 inches above the heat source.

2. Place the chicken pieces on the hot rack, skin side down. When seared, turn and grill the pieces bone side down, until light golden.

3. Remove the chicken from the grill and cover the rack with a layer of heavy-duty broiler foil. Puncture the foil to make plenty of ventilation holes.

4. Place the chicken on the foil, skin side down, and generously spoon on the barbecue sauce. Grill until the sauce is set. Then turn the pieces over, sauce the skin side, and grill bone side down.

5. Continue saucing and turning until all the pieces are done, about 50 to 60 minutes. To test for doneness, insert the tip of a sharp knife into the largest piece of chicken breast. If the juices run clear, it's done.

Yield: 3 cups sauce
Serves: 4 to 6

JERRY WOOD'S PERSONAL FAVORITE BARBECUED CHICKEN

North Carolina native Jerry Wood is president of Brook-wood Farms, a super-successful manufacturer of barbe-cued pork for commercial distribution. Obviously an avid barbecue enthusiast, he shares this personal favorite for chicken barbecue. "With this recipe," Jerry says, "you can do no wrong!"

1 cup ketchup

1 cup cider vinegar

1 cup water

4 tablespoons light brown sugar, packed

½ cup prepared mustard (ball-park variety)

¼ pound (1 stick) unsalted butter

2 teaspoons salt, or to taste

1 teaspoon cayenne pepper

¼ cup Worcestershire sauce

*8 to 10 pounds chicken, cut into serving
    pieces*

TO PREPARE THE SAUCE

In a 2-quart saucepan, combine all the ingredients through the Worcestershire sauce and cook together, uncovered, until somewhat thickened, about 30 minutes. Set aside until you are ready to barbecue.

TO BARBECUE THE CHICKEN

1. When the fire is ready, position the rack 5 inches above the heat source.

2. Place the chicken pieces on the hot rack, skin side down. When seared, turn and grill the pieces bone side down, until light golden.

3. Remove the chicken from the grill and cover the grill with a layer of heavy-duty broiler foil. Puncture the foil to make plenty of ventilation holes.

4. Place the chicken on the foil, skin side down, and generously spoon on the barbecue sauce. Grill until the sauce is set. Then turn the pieces over, sauce the skin side, and grill bone side down.

5. Continue saucing and turning until all the pieces are done, about 50 to 60 minutes. To test for doneness, insert the tip of a sharp knife into the largest piece of chicken breast. If the juices run clear, it's done.

Yield: 1 quart sauce
Serves: 8 to 10

ANTHONY'S SICILIAN BARBECUED CHICKEN

This is a very special relish-type barbecue recipe that I discovered in a rather unusual way. En route to judge a chile contest, I struck up a conversation with the limousine driver, a retired New York policeman, who loved to cook. When he found that I also loved to cook and actually wrote cookbooks, he offered to share his all-time favorite recipe, which just happens to be a very flavorful Italian-style chicken barbecue sauce that is also wonderful as a relish on cheese and crackers when you're in need of a creative snack. Anthony says he can never make enough of this sauce.

1 tablespoon vegetable oil

1 medium onion, finely chopped

¼ cup finely minced parsley

1 clove garlic, finely minced

½ cup dark brown sugar, packed

1 cup water

3 to 4 large ripe tomatoes, peeled, seeded
    and chopped or puréed, enough to
    measure 2 cups

½ fresh lemon, juiced

½ fresh orange, juiced

1 teaspoon red wine vinegar

1 tablespoon paprika

1 teaspoon salt, or to taste

¼ teaspoon freshly ground black pepper

6 pounds chicken, cut into serving pieces

TO PREPARE THE SAUCE

1. In a heavy saucepan heat the oil over medium heat. Add the onion, parsley and garlic and sauté until the onions are golden.

2. In the meantime, dissolve the brown sugar in the water.

3. Add this sugar-water mixture and the tomatoes to the onion mixture in the saucepan and cook, uncovered, until thickened, about 30 minutes.

4. Add the remaining ingredients through the pepper and cook until the sauce has thickened to the consistency of jam. Set aside until you are ready to barbecue.

TO BARBECUE THE CHICKEN

1. When the fire is ready, position the rack 5 inches above the heat source.

2. Place the chicken pieces on the hot rack, skin side down. When seared, turn and grill the pieces bone side down, until light golden.

3. Remove the chicken from the grill and cover the grill with a layer of heavy-duty broiler foil. Puncture the foil to make plenty of ventilation holes.

4. Place the chicken on the foil, skin side down, and generously spoon on the barbecue sauce. Grill until the sauce is set. Then turn the pieces over, sauce the skin side, and grill bone side down.

5. Continue saucing and turning until all the pieces are done, about 50 to 60 minutes. To test for doneness, insert the tip of a sharp knife into the largest piece of chicken breast. If the juices run clear, it's done.

Yield: 3¼ cups sauce
Serves: 4 to 6

SOUTHWEST CHICKEN BBQ

An easy-to-do hot, spicy barbecue sauce to use when time is short. It's great on pork or beef ribs, too.

1 cup ketchup

5 tablespoons unsalted butter, if available. Or use salted butter and omit the salt listed below.

¼ cup strong black coffee

3 tablespoons Worcestershire sauce

1 to 2 tablespoons pure ground hot chile or chile caribe (crushed red chile)

1 tablespoon dark brown sugar, packed

¼ teaspoon salt, or to taste

3 to 4 pounds chicken, cut into serving pieces

TO PREPARE THE SAUCE

In a 2-quart saucepan combine all the ingredients through the salt and allow the sauce to simmer, uncovered, over medium heat for 10 to 15 minutes. Set aside until you are ready to barbecue.

TO BARBECUE THE CHICKEN

1. When the fire is ready, position the rack 5 inches above the heat source.

2. Place the chicken pieces on the hot rack, skin side down. When seared, turn and grill the pieces bone side down, until light golden.

3. Remove the chicken from the grill and cover the grill with a layer of heavy-duty broiler foil. Puncture the foil to make plenty of ventilation holes.

4. Place the chicken on the foil, skin side down, and generously spoon on the barbecue sauce. Grill until the sauce is set. Then turn the pieces over, sauce the skin side, and grill bone side down.

5. Continue saucing and turning until all the pieces are done, about 50 to 60 minutes. To test for doneness, insert the tip of a sharp knife into the largest piece of chicken breast. If the juices run clear, it's done.

Yield: 1½ cups sauce
Serves: 3 to 4

OUTRAGEOUS HAM STEAK

One steamy hot night in Georgia, I was privileged to sample the recipe of one of my favorite friends, professional cook Nathalie Dupree, who manages the cooking schools at Rich's Department Stores in Atlanta.

¾ cup ketchup

¼ cup cider vinegar

2 teaspoons Worcestershire sauce

¼ teaspoon hot pepper sauce, or to taste

2 tablespoons prepared mustard (ball-park variety)

¼ cup molasses or dark brown sugar (packed)

½ teaspoon salt

2 center-cut fully cooked ham steaks, 1 inch thick

TO PREPARE THE SAUCE

Combine all the ingredients through the salt in a 2-quart saucepan and simmer, uncovered, over medium heat for 15 minutes. Set aside until you are ready to barbecue.

TO BARBECUE THE HAM

1. To rid the ham of excess salt and fat, first place the steaks in a large skillet in water to cover. Parboil them over medium-high heat for about 5 minutes. Pour off the water. Remove the steaks from the skillet and pat them dry with a paper towel. (This step is necessary *only* if you use country ham.)

2. Place the steaks in a large roasting pan and pour the sauce over them. Marinate the ham in the sauce for 20 minutes at room temperature.

3. Remove the steaks from the pan, reserving the sauce. With a sharp knife, cut slashes in the fat around the edges of the steaks, to prevent their curling during grilling.

4. When the fire is ready, grease the rack with a small piece of ham fat and position it 3 to 4 inches above the heat source. Place the ham steaks on the grill, and baste and turn frequently as they cook. The steaks will be done in 25 to 30 minutes.

Yield: 1¼ cups sauce
Serves: 4

DOWN HOME LOUISIANA BARBECUED SHRIMP

I was given this recipe while visiting friends in Cajun country. They prepare the sauce one week in advance of the barbecue and then refrigerate it. I suggest you do the same—the flavors will have melded just the right amount during that time. Reheat the sauce when barbecue day arrives. Keep extra bowls of it on the table so guests who want more can serve themselves. Hush Puppies (page 77), Barbecued Baked Beans (page 74), and coleslaw or a mixed green salad, and for dessert the Texas Pecan Cake (page 80) make for a super backyard party. In the South, gallons of sweetened iced tea and beer are served to quench the thirst.

2 cups ketchup

1 cup water

½ cup cider vinegar

¾ cup granulated sugar

2 cloves garlic, minced

½ cup finely chopped onion

½ cup finely diced green pepper

½ cup finely diced celery

¼ cup finely minced parsley

Juice and rind of 1 lemon

⅛ teaspoon liquid hot pepper sauce, or more to taste

1½ tablespoons Worcestershire sauce

1½ teaspoons liquid smoke

½ teaspoon each dried basil, dried oregano and ground cinnamon

1 tablespoon bacon drippings

Salt to taste

5 pounds large shrimp, peeled and deveined

TO PREPARE THE SAUCE

1. In a 3-quart saucepan combine all the ingredients through the bacon drippings. Cook, uncovered, over medium heat, stirring frequently, until contents are reduced to 1 quart (4 cups), approximately 35 to 50 minutes. Taste and add salt if necessary.

2. Allow the sauce to cool, then cover and refrigerate for 1 week before using.

TO BARBECUE THE SHRIMP

1. Allow the sauce to come to room temperature, then place it and the shrimp in a large bowl and marinate for 1 hour. Stir the shrimp in the sauce once or twice during the marinating period.

2. While the shrimp are marinating, prepare the grill. When the fire is ready, position the rack 4 inches above the heat source, then cover it with a layer of heavy-duty broiler foil. Puncture the foil to make ventilation holes.

3. Place the shrimp in a hinged wire grill basket or spread the shrimp evenly on the prepared rack. Allow them to cook 1 minute, then brush them with the barbecue sauce and turn. Brush again with more sauce. Shrimp cook quickly, and should be ready within 5 minutes.

Yield: 1 quart sauce
Serves: 4 to 6

FLORIDA SHRIMP

Way down south in sunny Florida, the orange influence shines, and for good reason. This sauce is as superb on chicken or ribs as it is on shrimp.

⅓ cup freshly squeezed lemon juice
⅓ cup freshly squeezed orange juice
⅓ cup chili sauce (ketchup type)
1 clove garlic, minced
1 teaspoon dry mustard
1 tablespoon Worcestershire sauce
¼ cup honey
¼ cup vegetable oil
¼ teaspoon paprika
Salt and freshly ground black pepper, to taste
1½ pounds large shrimp, peeled and deveined

TO PREPARE THE SAUCE

Combine all the ingredients through the salt and pepper in a blender and blend thoroughly. Set the sauce aside until you are ready to barbecue the shrimp.

TO BARBECUE THE SHRIMP

1. When you are ready to barbecue place the sauce and the shrimp in a large bowl and marinate for 1 hour. Stir the shrimp in the sauce once or twice during the marinating period.

2. While the shrimp are marinating, prepare the grill. When the fire is ready, position the rack 4 inches above the heat source, then cover it with a layer of heavy-duty broiler foil. Puncture the foil to make ventilation holes.

3. Place the shrimp in a hinged wire grill basket or spread the shrimp evenly on the prepared rack. Allow them to cook 1 minute, then brush them with the barbecue sauce and turn. Brush again with more sauce. Shrimp cook quickly, and should be ready within 5 minutes.

Yield: 1½ cups sauce
Serves: 2 to 3

INDOOR BARBECUE

No matter the time, the season or the circumstance, you can savor the saucy goodness of succulent barbecues. Don't let bad weather or the absence of a grill, backyard or patio keep you from this mouthwatering enjoyment. You can still approximate the flavor of barbecue in your oven.

The following recipes were chosen for this section because they work particularly well indoors but most can be prepared outdoors. If you wish to try any of the recipes in the outdoor section in your oven broiler, go ahead. Just be sure not to baste the meat with the barbecue sauce until the final few minutes of cooking. Otherwise you will wind up with a crispy outside long before the inside of the meat is cooked.

BARBECUED PORK

This is a quick and easy barbecue taste when time won't allow for long, slow cooking. And it's more authentic than a hamburger.

1 pound coarsely ground pork
2 teaspoons minced garlic
1 medium onion, finely chopped
1 cup sauce from Jane's Best Barbecued
    Ribs (page 20) or your favorite
6 whole-wheat hamburger buns, split,
    lightly buttered and toasted

1. In a bowl mix the pork with the garlic and onion.

2. In a heavy skillet crumble the pork mixture and sauté over medium heat until the pork is thoroughly cooked. Drain well.

3. Return the pork to the skillet and add the barbecue sauce. Stir to combine well then simmer gently over medium heat for 15 minutes.

4. Place the split, toasted buns on serving plates and let each person spoon on the barbecued pork.

Serves: 2 to 3

BERNIE'S ORIENTAL RIBS

I savored these uniquely flavorful ribs one night quite by surprise. That day I had just completed a radio interview. Before the interview, I mentioned I was heading for the Catskills for relaxation and the announcer replied, "On the way, you really must try Bernie's Restaurant." He said that he knew I'd love it, and I did!

6 pounds baby back pork ribs

½ cup Hoisin sauce*, or more to taste

½ cup mashed, black bean sauce*, or more to taste

1 tablespoon Sang Chow sauce* (optional)

18 ounces tomato purée

1½ teaspoons ground ginger

1½ teaspoons Chinese Five Spice Powder*

1½ teaspoons ground anise

10 ounces (⅝ cup) granulated sugar

2 tablespoons puréed fresh garlic

1 tablespoon Tomato Shade*

3 tablespoons salt, more or less, to taste

1 tablespoon dry sherry

1. Preheat the oven to 400° F.

2. Cut the ribs into serving-size pieces and place them in a glass dish.

3. In a bowl, mix all the other ingredients thoroughly. Spread the mixture on the ribs and let them sit for 4 to 6 hours at room temperature, or, covered, overnight in the refrigerator if you prefer.

4. Set a rack over a roasting pan with 1 to 1½ inches of water in it. Remove the ribs from the marinade and place them on the rack. Cook the ribs until they are done, about 30 to 40 minutes. Turn and baste them every 10 minutes during the cooking.

Yield: 2½ cups sauce
Serves: 6

*Can be purchased at Oriental food markets. Tomato Shade is the coloring traditionally used by Chinese cooks to give ribs their characteristic color. It adds no flavor, so don't worry if you can't find it locally.

BARBECUED COUNTRY-STYLE PORK RIBS

This flavorful recipe hails from California and adds a different twist to traditional barbecue. Make the Sour Cream Sauce while the ribs are marinating so you can chill it before serving it alongside at the table.

1 cup red wine
1 cup red wine vinegar
1 carrot, peeled and grated
1 small onion, peeled and stuck with
    3 whole cloves
¼ teaspoon thyme
2 cloves garlic, minced
3 pounds country-style pork ribs, in
    individual pieces
1 teaspoon salt
Freshly ground black pepper to taste
1 recipe Sour Cream Sauce (recipe follows)

FOR THE MARINADE

1. Combine the ingredients through the garlic in a large glass or ceramic bowl.

2. Sprinkle the ribs with salt and pepper and place them in the marinade, uncovered, for 2 hours at room temperature, or, covered, overnight in the refrigerator. Turn the ribs occasionally.

TO BARBECUE THE RIBS

1. Preheat the oven for 15 minutes at 450° F.

2. Remove the ribs from the marinade, reserving ½ cup for the Sour Cream Sauce.

3. Place the ribs on a rack placed over a roasting pan and cook for 10 minutes per side.

4. Remove the pan from the oven. Reduce the heat to 350° F. Spoon on the marinade, coating the ribs well. Return the pan to the oven.

5. Every 10 minutes, turn and baste the ribs.

6. When the sauce forms a rich glaze (about 45 minutes), remove the ribs from the oven and transfer to a serving platter. Serve with the Sour Cream Sauce.

BBQ DIP

SOUR CREAM SAUCE

2 tablespoons unsalted butter
2 small onions, finely minced
½ cup reserved marinade
¼ teaspoon freshly ground black pepper
¾ cup sour cream, at room temperature
¼ cup finely minced parsley

1. Melt the butter in a small skillet over medium heat. Add the onions and sauté them until they are transparent. Add the marinade, increase the heat, and bring the mixture to a boil. Reduce the heat and simmer, uncovered, until the liquid is reduced by one-third.

2. Add the pepper and stir in the sour cream. Remove the mixture from the heat as soon as the sour cream is well incorporated (do *not* boil), and stir in the parsley. Refrigerate this sauce while you cook the ribs.

NEW ENGLAND MAPLE BARBECUED PORK

Tom Boyhan adds maple syrup to his winning sauce and uses it to marinate cubes of pork shoulder. Then the pork is combined on skewers with chunks of navel oranges and sections of bell peppers. The resulting kabobs won him the title of King at the 1979 New York State Pork Cookout. Make the sauce at least a day in advance of your barbecue. Keep it refrigerated in a covered container until you are ready to use it.

2 cups ketchup

1½ cups pure maple syrup

½ cup cider vinegar

½ cup fresh orange juice

2 tablespoons Worcestershire sauce

2 teaspoons salt

2 tablespoons minced onion

½ teaspoon liquid smoke (optional)

2 to 2½ pounds boneless pork shoulder, cut in 1½-inch cubes

2 unpeeled navel oranges, cut in wedges

3 green bell peppers, steamed, seeded and cut in 1½-inch cubes

12 bamboo skewers, 7 to 8 inches long

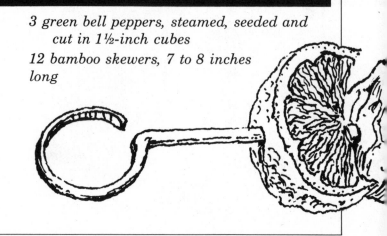

TO PREPARE THE SAUCE

1. Combine ketchup, maple syrup, vinegar, orange juice, Worcestershire sauce, salt and onion in a 2-quart saucepan. Simmer, uncovered, over medium heat for 15 minutes.

2. Add the liquid smoke, stir, and set aside until you are ready to marinate the meat.

TO BARBECUE THE PORK

1. Place the pork cubes in a shallow glass bowl or baking dish. Pour the sauce over the cubes. Stir, making sure all sides of the meat are covered with the sauce.

2. Marinate for 1 to 2 hours at room temperature or, covered, overnight in the refrigerator.

3. Preheat the oven to 450° F.

4. On each skewer place a wedge of orange, then alternating pork cubes and green pepper cubes.

5. Place the kabobs on a rack in a shallow baking pan and roast in the oven (not the broiler) for 10 minutes, turning occasionally.

6. Reduce the heat to 350° F, baste the kabobs, and continue to cook for about 20 minutes, turning and basting again after 10 minutes. When done, the sauce will have formed a thick rich brown glaze.

Yield: 1 quart sauce
Serves: 6

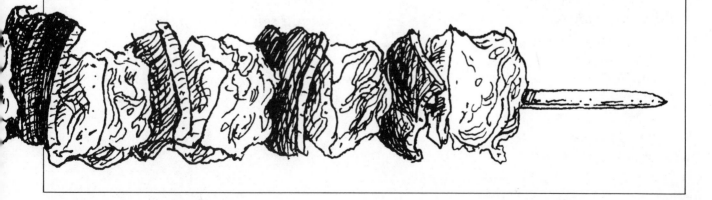

YANKEE BRISKET PULLED BARBECUE

A Yankee version of the famous pit-cooked "pulled" barbecue, this is a super prepare-ahead meal. Sylvia Carter, food writer for *Newsday* in New York, introduced me to this finger lickin' good recipe. Serve with steamed soft buns, large garlicky dill pickles, coleslaw and baked beans. A word of warning: make lots! There is seldom any left. It is one of the best for large gatherings, as it waits patiently for buffet service and seems to somehow improve with the waiting.

4 pounds beef brisket or chuck roast (pork shoulder may also be used)

3½-ounce bottle liquid smoke

2 cups chopped onions

¼ cup cider vinegar

¼ cup dark brown sugar, packed

2 tablespoons Dusseldorf mustard or any spicy brown mustard, or yellow mustard

1 tablespoon dark molasses

¼ teaspoon cayenne pepper

¼ teaspoon liquid hot pepper sauce

3 tablespoons Worcestershire sauce

1 cup ketchup

½ cup chili sauce (ketchup type)

½ lemon, sliced

1 tablespoon salt, more or less, to taste

¼ teaspoon freshly ground black pepper

1. Preheat the oven to 325° F.

2. Put the meat on a rack in a roasting pan, fat side up, and pour the liquid smoke around it. Seal the pan with foil and place in the oven. Roast the brisket for 4 hours, or until it is very tender, turning once. Uncover the meat for the last 30 minutes to brown.

3. Remove the meat from the oven and let it cool. Wrap it in plastic and refrigerate. Pour the pan juices and fat into a glass jar or bowl, cover and refrigerate.

4. The next day, remove the meat from the refrigerator and trim away any extra fat. Pull the meat into small shreds (this is called "pulling").

5. Remove the hardened fat from the pan juices. In a large pot, melt 3 tablespoons of the hardened fat over medium heat, add the onions and sauté until tender. Add all the remaining ingredients and 1 cup of the pan juices. Stir well and simmer for 20 minutes over low heat.

6. Add the "pulled" meat to the sauce and simmer very slowly, uncovered, for 1 hour, stirring frequently. Add more pan juices, or water, if necessary, to keep the meat moist.

Serves: 8 to 12

BBQ
"PULLED" BARBECUE

This method prepares your meat for a delicious "pulled" barbecue. I prefer using beef brisket and beef round roasts, but pork shoulders and butts may be used. Here's how to do it in the oven or on top of the stove.

1. If you are cooking the meat in the oven, preheat it to 325° F.
2. Sprinkle the meat with salt and pepper to taste. Place it in a heavy pot. If you intend to cook the meat on a burner, add ½ cup water to the pot and cover tightly with a lid or aluminum foil. Cook on the lowest flame or heat setting possible. Check the meat periodically and add more water if necessary. If you are cooking the meat in the oven, you need not add water. Just cover tightly and place in the oven.
3. For either method, cook approximately 1 hour per pound of meat, or until the meat is fork tender and falls apart.
4. When the meat is done, remove it from the pot and allow it to cool. Trim any excess fat from the meat. For full "pulled" meat, pull meat into shreds with your hands or two forks. For partially "pulled" meat, pull the meat into 1-inch chunks.
5. Return the shredded meat to the pot, add your favorite sauce, allowing ½ cup sauce per pound of meat, or to taste, and cook, uncovered, over low heat. The barbecue should be heated through.

TEXAS BEEF BARBECUE

"Texas-class" all the way! I love to serve it with the sauce used in James Beal's Barbecued Ribs, page 22, alongside, but you can use your own favorite with it. Serve the meat charred but rare for a true Texas taste.

4 pounds top beef round, well trimmed

¼ cup lard

½ teaspoon chile caribe (crushed red chile)

½ cup boiling water

8 tablespoons unsalted butter

½ cup tarragon vinegar, or ½ cup cider
     vinegar plus 1 tablespoon fresh or
     1 teaspoon dried tarragon

1½ cups dry red wine

⅓ cup freshly grated onion

2 tablespoons Worcestershire sauce

1 large clove garlic, minced

1. Wipe the meat with a damp cloth then rub it with half the lard and all the chile caribe.

2. In a 1-quart saucepan boil the water. Add the remaining lard and all the butter. Allow them to melt, then add the rest of the ingredients and stir to mix.

3. Place the meat in a medium-size mixing bowl, and pour the sauce over it. Let the meat stand in the liquid for 4 hours at room temperature, or for 2 days, covered, in the refrigerator. Turn the meat from time to time so both sides absorb the marinade.

4. Preheat the broiler. Remove the meat from the marinade and place it on the broiler pan. Position the pan on the bottom rack of the broiler, as far as possible from the broiling unit, so the surface of the meat is 3 to 4 inches from the heat. Broil the meat for 15 minutes. Turn the meat and baste it generously with marinade, rubbing

the fat from the marinade over the surface of the meat. Broil another 15 minutes. Turn the meat and baste again thoroughly. Broil 15 minutes. At this point the meat will be rare. Baste the meat, remove it from the oven and allow it to rest for 15 minutes.

5. If a more well-done roast is desired, reduce the oven temperature to 325° F, and cook the roast in the oven for an additional 30 to 60 minutes, depending on the doneness preferred.

6. Serve with your choice of sauce at the table.

Serves: 6 to 8

Note: If a broiler is not available, roast the meat in a preheated 450° F oven for 30 minutes, basting frequently. Turn the meat, reduce the temperature to 325° F and cook for 2 hours, basting every 20 minutes, or until the meat tests done with a meat thermometer (internal temperature of 150° F).

BBQ

AMY'S SLOPPY JOE'S

My daughter, Amy, and her friends have made these a frequent request. Spicy and saucy, they're wonderful on fresh soft whole-wheat buns.

1 pound lean ground beef, cold or at room temperature
¼ cup finely diced onion
1 clove garlic, minced
¼ cup ketchup
2 teaspoons pure ground mild red chile
1 teaspoon prepared mustard (ball-park variety)
1 teaspoon Worcestershire sauce
¼ teaspoon liquid smoke (optional)
½ teaspoon celery salt
6 fresh whole-wheat hamburger buns

In a large skillet, crumble the hamburger and cook over medium heat. As it cooks, add the remaining ingredients through the celery salt, stirring to mix well with the hamburger. When thoroughly cooked, spoon onto toasted whole-wheat hamburger buns and serve.

Yield: 6 sandwiches

JERRY'S BEEF BARBECUE

Since Jerry Wood feels that beef requires a different sauce from chicken or pork, I have added another of his favorites.

1 cup beef broth
3 cups ketchup
½ cup cider vinegar
¼ cup Worcestershire sauce
¼ cup light brown sugar, packed
2 teaspoons salt, or to taste
1 teaspoon liquid smoke (optional)
4½- to 6-pound chuck roast

TO PREPARE THE SAUCE

In a 2-quart saucepan, combine all the ingredients through the salt, and bring them to a simmer over medium heat. Reduce the heat to low and cook, uncovered, 30 minutes, until slightly thickened. Add the liquid smoke, if desired. Set the sauce aside to cool.

TO ROAST THE BEEF

1. In a large roasting pan marinate the roast in the sauce for 2 hours at room temperature. Turn the meat after an hour.

2. Preheat the oven to 325° F.

3. Remove the meat from the marinade and wipe off any extra sauce. Reserve the marinade. Place the meat in a clean casserole or roasting pan, cover it tightly (using foil if necessary), and cook for 3½ hours or until it is very tender. After 2 hours, turn the roast.

4. Uncover the meat and cook for another 30 minutes, basting with the reserved sauce, until it is nice and brown.

5. Remove the roast from the pan, allow it to cool for 15 minutes, then slice it thin, and serve with the reserved sauce.

Yield: 1 quart sauce
Serves: 6 to 8

JANE'S SPECIAL SWEET AND SOUR CHICKEN

This is one of the best summer weekend dishes around. The sauce is terrific as well as quick and easy to prepare. Serve this chicken with a creamy cole-slaw and foil-wrapped, grill-roasted corn on the cob.

¾ cup ketchup

¾ cup apricot preserves

2 tablespoons white or cider vinegar

1 teaspoon Worcestershire sauce

1 tablespoon pure ground mild red chile

½ teaspoon salt

3 to 4 pounds chicken, cut into serving pieces

To Prepare the Sauce

1. In a 2-quart saucepan combine all the ingredients through the salt and cook over medium heat until the mixture comes to a boil. Stir the sauce occasionally to prevent it from sticking.

2. Reduce the heat to low and simmer, uncovered, for 5 minutes. Set the sauce aside until you are ready to cook the chicken—or once it has cooled, marinate the chicken in the sauce for 1 to 2 hours at room temperature for even better flavor.

To Barbecue the Chicken

1. Adjust the broiler rack so that the chicken will be 3 to 4 inches from the heat.

2. Preheat the broiler.

3. Lay the chicken pieces on the rack of a broiler, skin side up. (If you want, cover the rack with heavy-duty broiler foil punctured with holes.) Broil for 20 minutes. Turn the chicken, baste it with the sauce, and cook for 15 minutes. Then turn and baste again. Baste and turn every 5 minutes until the chicken is done, in another 15 to 25 minutes.

Yield: 1½ cups sauce
Serves: 2

SWEET SOUTHERN CHICKEN

Mississippians like barbecue, too! This recipe has a sweet, savory, tart taste—it's the lemon that makes it special. Given to me by a highly respected friend in the fine-food field, I bet you will want to add this one to your "favorites" file. Once you're hooked, you'll want to try it on other meats. It's good on fish, too!

1 cup ketchup

2 tablespoons honey

3 tablespoons lemon juice

1 tablespoon Worcestershire sauce

4 large cloves garlic, finely minced

4 tablespoons bacon drippings

1 small lemon, sliced thin, seeds removed

Liquid hot pepper sauce to taste

Salt and freshly ground black pepper, to taste

½ teaspoon liquid smoke (optional)

3 pounds chicken, cut into serving pieces

To Prepare the Sauce

1. In a 2-quart enamel saucepan combine all the ingredients through the salt and pepper and bring to a boil over medium-high heat, stirring occasionally. When it is thoroughly blended, in about 20 minutes, add the liquid smoke and set the sauce aside until you are ready to cook the chicken. Or for even better flavor, marinate the chicken in the sauce for 1 to 2 hours at room temperature.

To Barbecue the Chicken

1. Adjust the broiler rack of your oven so that the surface of the chicken will be 3 to 4 inches from the heat.

2. Preheat the broiler.

3. Lay the chicken pieces on the rack of a broiler pan, skin side up. (If you want, cover the rack with heavy-duty broiler foil punctured with holes.) Broil for 20 minutes. Turn the chicken, baste it with the sauce, and cook for 15 minutes. Then turn it and baste again. Baste and turn every 5 minutes until the chicken is done, in another 15 to 25 minutes.

Yield: 1½ cups sauce
Serves: 2 to 3

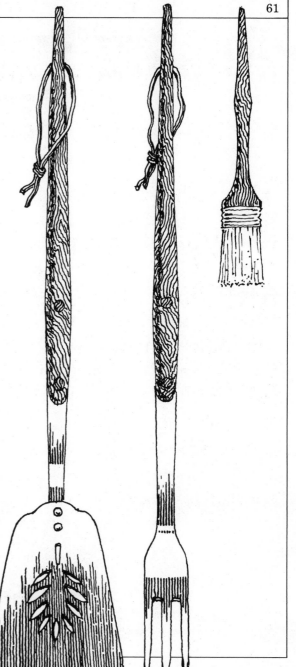

ADDIE'S TEXAS BARBECUED CHICKEN

This dish is from deep in the heart of Texas. My favorite sister-in-law treated me to it for the first time more than twenty years ago, and to this day I think it's the best. Addie, who hailed from Arkansas as a kid, says the secret is in using the melted unsalted butter and the freshest possible ingredients. Addie also introduced me to her famous potato salad. I still make my potato salad this same way and have included her recipe on page 73. All you need with this barbecued chicken and Addie's potato salad is a relish tray. Then just sit back and wait for compliments.

½ cup cider vinegar

2 tablespoons light brown sugar, packed

1 tablespoon prepared mustard (ball-park variety)

1½ teaspoons salt, or to taste

½ teaspoon freshly ground black pepper

2 tablespoons fresh lemon juice

1 cup finely diced onion

½ cup (2 sticks) unsalted butter, cut into 6 pieces

15-ounce can tomato sauce

2 tablespoons Worcestershire sauce

1½ teaspoons liquid smoke (optional)

¼ teaspoon each dried sage, basil, rosemary and thyme, or ½ teaspoon of each fresh herb, minced

6 pounds chicken, cut into serving pieces

To Prepare the Sauce

1. In a 2-quart saucepan combine the vinegar, brown sugar, mustard, salt, pepper, lemon, onion and butter. Bring the mixture to a boil over high heat. Reduce the heat to medium and simmer for 20 minutes, uncovered. Stir occasionally.

2. Add the tomato sauce, Worcestershire sauce and liquid smoke (if you are using it). Simmer for 15 minutes longer, again stirring occasionally.

3. Add the herbs, reduce the heat to low, and cook the sauce for 5 minutes. Remove the sauce from the heat, cool, cover, and refrigerate until you are ready to barbecue.

To Barbecue the Chicken

1. Adjust the broiler rack of your oven so the chicken will be 4 inches from the heat.

2. Preheat the broiler.

3. Lay the chicken pieces on the rack of a broiler pan, skin side up. (If you want, cover the rack with heavy-duty broiler foil punctured with holes.) Broil for 20 minutes. Turn the chicken, baste it with the sauce, and cook for 15 minutes. Then turn it and baste again. Baste and turn every 5 minutes until the chicken is done, in another 15 to 25 minutes.

Yield: 3½ cups sauce
Serves: 6

Note: As a sauce variation, omit the herbs and add:

3 whole green chiles, finely chopped

¼ teaspoon ground ginger

¼ teaspoon ground cinnamon

Several drops of liquid hot pepper sauce, or to taste

ORANGE BARBECUED HAM

This sweet sauce is terrific on poultry as well as ham. A salad of peeled sliced oranges and red onions served on lettuce leaves with poppy-seed/honey dressing is delicious with it along with baked sweet potatoes.

A bone-in ready-to-eat ham should be cooked at 14 minutes per pound. A boneless ham will take longer—30 minutes per pound.

½ cup honey
½ cup dry red wine
2 teaspoons freshly grated orange rind
½ cup freshly squeezed orange juice
2 teaspoons unsalted butter
2 teaspoons snipped chives
Salt and freshly ground pepper, to taste
5- to 7-pound ready-to-eat ham

TO PREPARE THE SAUCE

In a 2-quart enamel saucepan combine all the ingredients through the salt and pepper and cook, uncovered, over medium heat for 20 minutes. Set aside until you are ready to cook the ham.

TO BAKE THE HAM

1. Preheat the oven to 400° F.

2. Place the ham in a large roasting pan and then in the oven.

3. After 20 minutes, reduce the heat to 325° F. After another 30 minutes, start basting the ham at 20-minute intervals.

4. After 2 hours roasting time, remove the ham from the oven. Cut off the rind and all but ¼ inch of fat; score the fat and baste with the sauce.

5. Return the ham to the oven and baste every 5 minutes until done.

Yield: 1¾ cups sauce
Serves: 10 to 12

MUSTARD BARBECUED HAM

One regional sauce, popular with the western South Carolinians, is this mustard-base version.

¾ cup water
3 tablespoons finely minced onion
1 medium clove garlic, finely minced
1 cup prepared mustard (ball-park variety)
1 teaspoon dry mustard
3 tablespoons ketchup-style chile sauce
2 tablespoons plus 1 teaspoon sugar
2 teaspoons honey
1 tablespoon Worcestershire sauce
⅛ teaspoon freshly ground white pepper
¼ teaspoon freshly ground black pepper
½ teaspoon ground hot red pepper
5- to 7-pound ready-to-eat ham

TO PREPARE THE SAUCE

1. In a 2-quart saucepan place the water, onion and garlic, and bring to a boil over medium heat.

2. Reduce the heat to low and add the remaining ingredients, through the red pepper, whisking thoroughly to combine.

3. Continue to cook for 15 minutes. Remove the sauce from the heat. If you wish to refrigerate it, let it cool to room temperature.

TO BAKE THE HAM

1. Preheat the oven to 400° F.

2. Place the ham in a large roasting pan and then in the oven. After 20 minutes, reduce the heat to 325° F.

3. After another 30 minutes, start basting the ham at 20-minute intervals.

4. Forty-five minutes before the cooking time is up, remove the ham from the oven. Cut off the rind and all but ¼ inch of fat; score the fat and baste with the sauce.

5. Return the ham to the oven and baste every 5 minutes until it is done. A bone-in ready-to-eat ham should be cooked 14 minutes per pound. A boneless ham will take longer—30 minutes per pound.

Yield: 2 cups sauce
Serves: 10 to 12

STEVE'S BERMUDA LAMB

Steve Mandler, an enthusiastic cook living in San Francisco, claims he created this from memories of many fabulous barbecues in Bermuda. There many of the cooks keep "hot" wine in the refrigerator for flavoring sauces. (To make "hot" wine, see the Note below.)

½ cup honey
¼ cup brown sugar, packed
¾ cup bottled chili sauce (ketchup variety)
3 tablespoons Worcestershire sauce
½ teaspoon finely minced garlic
¼ cup minced onion
½ cup flat beer
¼ teaspoon cayenne or "hot" wine (see Note)
4 pounds lamb riblets

TO PREPARE THE SAUCE

In a heavy 1-quart saucepan combine all the ingredients through the cayenne pepper (or "hot" wine). Bring the mixture to a boil over low heat and simmer, uncovered, for 10 minutes. Set the sauce aside until you are ready to barbecue the lamb.

TO BARBECUE THE LAMB

1. Preheat the oven to 450° F.

2. Place the riblets on a rack in a shallow baking pan and sear 10 minutes on each side. (You can line the rack with heavy-duty broiler foil, if you like. Puncture plenty of holes in it for ventilation.)

3. Reduce the heat to 350° F, baste the riblets with the sauce, and continue cooking for between 20 to 30 minutes, basting and turning every 10 minutes.

Yield: 2 cups sauce
Serves: 4

Note: To make "hot" wine, steep ¼ cup crushed red chile peppers in ½ cup red wine for 3 days, in the refrigerator. Substitute 1 teaspoon of this wine for the cayenne pepper.

BIG FISH BARBECUE

Up North 'most anyone worth having fun with loves barbecue as much as Southerners do. I like using this Northern sauce on fish best of all.

2 tablespoons vegetable oil
2 cups finely chopped onions
½ cup chicken or beef stock
1 cup peeled and chopped fresh tomatoes, or
    canned Italian plum tomatoes
4 tablespoons freshly squeezed lemon juice
3 tablespoons light brown sugar
3 tablespoons Worcestershire sauce
2 tablespoons dry mustard
1 tablespoon salt
Freshly ground black pepper to taste
Dash of liquid hot pepper sauce
3 to 4 pounds fresh fish steaks such
    as halibut, salmon, or swordfish,
    1 inch thick

TO PREPARE THE SAUCE

1. Place the oil in a 1-quart saucepan over medium heat. Add the onions and sauté them until they are transparent.

2. Add the remaining ingredients through the hot pepper sauce and bring the mixture to a boil. Lower the heat and simmer about 30 minutes. Set the sauce aside until you are ready to barbecue.

TO BARBECUE THE FISH

1. Preheat the broiler and position the rack 5 inches below the heat source. Line a broiling pan with aluminum foil.

2. Place the fish in the broiling pan and set it on the broiler rack. Allow the fish to cook 1 minute, then turn it. Spoon on the sauce. Broil for 4 minutes. Then turn the fish again and sauce the second side.

3. Fish cooks quickly and will fall apart if turned too many times, so do not turn the steaks more than twice. They should take no longer than 10 to 12 minutes. The fish is cooked when it flakes easily with a fork.

Yield: 1¾ cups sauce
Serves: 6 to 8

SAN FRANCISCO BARBECUED FISH

A sweet-tart, slightly smoky sauce to serve with any full-flavored fish such as trout, sturgeon, or tuna.

2 ¼-inch-thick slices of slab bacon, cut into narrow strips and diced

2 medium onions, finely chopped

3 large cloves garlic, minced

16 ounces tomato sauce

6 tablespoons brown sugar, packed

¼ cup white wine vinegar

4 tablespoons plus 2 teaspoons fresh lemon juice

10 ounces flat beer

1 tablespoon Worcestershire sauce

1½ tablespoons tamari or soy sauce

1 teaspoon each ground ginger, ground allspice, freshly ground nutmeg, and celery seed

½ teaspoon cayenne pepper, or chile pequin, more or less to taste

1 tablespoon liquid smoke (optional)

Salt to taste

2½ pounds any of the above fish fillets or 3 to 4 pounds baby red snapper, whole

To Prepare the Sauce

1. In a skillet, sauté the bacon over medium heat until the fat is transparent. Add the onions and garlic and continue cooking until the onion is softened but not browned. Transfer this mixture to a 2-quart saucepan and add the remaining ingredients through the cayenne pepper.

2. Bring the mixture to the boiling point over medium heat. Reduce the heat and simmer, uncovered, for 30 minutes. Turn off the heat, add the liquid smoke, if desired, stir, and let the sauce cool. Taste, add salt and adjust the seasonings.

3. Set the sauce aside until you are ready to barbecue the fish.

To Barbecue the Fish

1. Preheat the oven to 450° F.

2. Place the oven rack 4 to 6 inches from the top of the oven.

3. Line a shallow baking pan with foil. Place the fish in the pan and cook in the oven for 5 minutes before basting with the sauce.

4. Baste the fish with the sauce occasionally, but only turn the fish once. Cook for 10 minutes per inch of thickness.

Yield: 3½ cups sauce
Serves: 4 to 6

Note: You can also broil the fish. Just be sure it doesn't cook too quickly and dry out.

ACCOMPANIMENTS

A collection of just-the-right dishes to serve up with your favorite barbecued meat or fish. Then, for a blissful ending to the feast, a super rich Fudge or Texas Pecan Cake. Who could ask for anything more?

CHUCKWAGON SALAD

Great picnic fare, but don't dress the salad until you get to where you're going.

---

1 clove garlic, cut in half

3 cups lettuce (preferably two or three types, for example a combination of romaine, watercress, and red leaf), torn into bite-size pieces

2 stalks celery, thinly sliced

Half a cucumber, peeled and thinly sliced

2 medium ripe tomatoes, cut in wedges

2 hardboiled eggs, sliced and diced

1 cup large lima beans, cooked and thoroughly drained (½ cup dry)

¼ cup blue-veined cheese, crumbled

¼ cup olive oil

2 tablespoons white wine vinegar

1 teaspoon salad herbs—a combination of thyme, tarragon and sweet basil

Salt and freshly ground black pepper, to taste

1. Rub a wooden salad bowl with the cut garlic, then discard the garlic.

2. Add the lettuce, celery, cucumber, tomatoes, eggs and lima beans to the bowl.

3. Blend the cheese, oil and vinegar together and pour the mixture over the salad ingredients. Toss lightly and season with the herbs and salt and pepper, to taste. Serve immediately.

Serves: 4 to 6

KAY'S LEXINGTON BARBECUE COLESLAW

To Kay Goldstein, a native of Lexington, North Carolina, now living in Georgia, "Lexington barbecue sauce *is* barbecue sauce." In Lexington, barbecue coleslaw is famous and is served with and on everything.

1 medium head white cabbage (2½ to 3 pounds)
3 tablespoons granulated sugar
1 cup cider vinegar
⅔ cup ketchup
½ cup water
⅛ teaspoon cayenne pepper
⅛ teaspoon chile caribe (crushed red chile)
¼ teaspoon freshly ground black pepper
¾ teaspoon salt, or to taste
Dash of liquid hot pepper sauce, or to taste

1. Grate or thinly slice the cabbage. If you won't be using it for a while, you can keep the cabbage crisp by placing it in cold water to cover for several hours, or until needed. Drain well before using.

2. In a small saucepan combine the sugar and vinegar and cook over medium heat until the sugar dissolves.

3. Whisk in the other ingredients and simmer over medium-high heat for 10 minutes. If the mixture seems too thick, thin with 1 tablespoon of warm water at a time until the proper consistency is reached.

4. Pour the warm sauce over the grated cabbage. Toss to combine thoroughly, and serve immediately.

Serves: 6

TEXAS POTATO SALAD

This recipe came to me by way of my sister-in-law, Addie. Once you try it, you'll never go back to your old recipe... 'cause this one's fantastic!

4 medium-size baking potatoes (Idaho or Russet), unpeeled

2 teaspoons salt

2 large eggs

2 tablespoons vinegar

3 tablespoons unsalted butter

4 tablespoons finely diced Spanish onion

6 tablespoons finely diced sweet gherkins

3 tablespoons juice from the sweet gherkins

½ cup mayonnaise

1 whole canned pimiento, sliced into ¼-inch strips

1 whole sweet gherkin

1. Over medium heat in a covered saucepan, cook the potatoes in water to cover mixed with 1 teaspoon of the salt until they are fork tender, about 20 minutes. Remove the pan from the heat, drain the potatoes, and replace the lid, allowing the potatoes to steam for 15 minutes.

2. Meanwhile, cook the eggs with the vinegar and the remaining 1 teaspoon salt in water to cover, until just done, about 10 minutes. Drain and run cold water over them to cool. Peel, slice and dice the eggs.

3. Peel the potatoes and return them to the cooking pot. Add the butter to the pot, cutting through the potatoes with a sharp knife to allow the butter to be absorbed. The potatoes should be in rough, medium-size chunks. Cover the pot and allow them to stand, off the heat, for 10 minutes. If the potatoes are not hot enough to melt the butter, place the pot, covered, over low heat for a few minutes.

4. Off the heat, add the diced eggs, onion, diced gherkins, gherkin juice, and mayonnaise and mix thoroughly.

5. Transfer the mixture to your favorite bowl, garnish with sliced pimiento and place the whole gherkin in the center.

Serves: 4 to 6

BARBECUED BAKED BEANS

The combination of flavors makes this a favorite baked-bean recipe of all times.

4 slices lean bacon, cut crosswise into thin strips
1 cup finely diced Spanish onion
1 large clove garlic, minced
1 pound cooked navy or pea beans, or one 16-ounce can brick-oven baked beans
¾ cup ketchup
1 cup dark brown sugar, packed
1 teaspoon mustard powder
1 tablespoon pure ground mild red chile

1. Preheat the oven to 325° F.

2. In a heavy skillet, sauté the bacon strips over medium-high heat until crisp. Add the onion and garlic, and continue cooking until the onion is transparent but not browned.

3. Transfer the bacon, onion and any fat that may have accumulated to a mixing bowl. Add the remaining ingredients and combine well. Pour the mixture into an ungreased 2-quart baking dish and bake uncovered at 325° F for 2½ to 3 hours.

Serves: 4

Note: The beans will keep up to 2 weeks in the refrigerator, but don't freeze them; freezing tends to change the texture and make the beans mushy.

CORN ON THE COB

This is the best possible way to cook and serve fresh corn! Try it once and you'll be hooked for life.

4 ears fresh corn, husks and silk intact
2 gallons salted water

1. If the corn is more than 2 hours from the stalk, soak it in salted water for 10 to 20 minutes before placing it on your outdoor grill.

2. About 20 minutes before your meal is ready to be served, place the ears of corn on the grill, rotating them frequently. The husks will get slightly charred.

3. Corn is done when the kernels emit water when pierced with the point of a sharp knife or a fork, in about 15 to 20 minutes. Husk corn (be careful, it's still hot!) and serve immediately.

Serves: 4

Note: If corn "fresh off the stalk" is not available, the flavor of "tired" corn can be freshened by cooking the husked corn in a solution of 2 tablespoons sugar, ½ teaspoon salt and ¼ cup dried milk to each cup of water. Drain the corn well before serving.

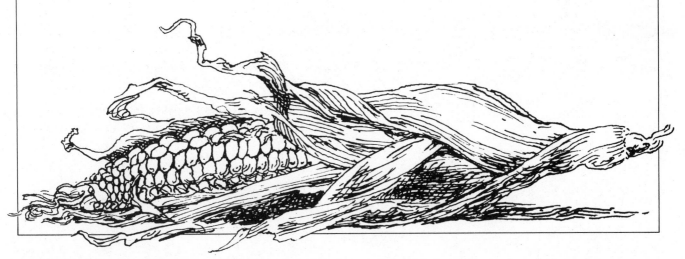

BARBECUED CHEESE

This tasty cheese dish bears a similarity to Swiss Raclette, which is the name both of a cheese and of the dish in which it is cooked. A wheel of Raclette is placed in a cast-iron skillet and a metal spike is inserted in the cheese to hold it steady. The skillet is placed over the fire and as the cheese slowly melts, it is scraped from the pan wheel with a sharp knife and served with fresh homemade bread or crackers.

½ wheel Raclette or Appenzell cheese
¼ cup virgin olive oil
1 to 2 teaspoons dried oregano

1. Brush the wheel of cheese with the olive oil and sprinkle with the oregano.

2. Place the cheese on a solid griddle or in a large cast-iron frying pan over an open fire, grill or a fire pit. If you are cooking indoors, place the griddle on a burner over medium heat. As the cheese melts, scrape it into the pan with a wooden knife or spatula, adding more oil and oregano if needed.

3. Serve the cheese directly from the pan on hot fresh bread and accompany it with red wine.

Serves: 10

NORMA JEAN'S HUSH PUPPIES

These hush puppies, a recipe from McEwen, Tennessee, are sheer heaven, the best I've ever encountered. When camping, I've even taken the dry ingredients mixed together so I could whip them up in the woods. They're terrific with any kind of barbecue.

1 quart peanut oil, for frying hush puppies
2 cups white cornmeal
1 tablespoon flour
½ teaspoon baking soda
1 teaspoon baking powder
2 teaspoons granulated sugar
1½ teaspoons salt
1 cup buttermilk
1 small onion, finely minced
1 egg, beaten

1. In a deep-fat fryer, preheat the oil to 375° F.

2. Combine all the other ingredients, adding the egg last. Mix well and drop, a tablespoonful at a time, into the hot fat. Do not overcrowd.

3. When done, in about 3 minutes, the hush puppies will turn golden brown and float to the top. Remove them from the oil with a slotted spoon or tongs and drain thoroughly on paper towels.

4. Serve the hush puppies warm.

Yield: twenty-four 1-inch hush puppies
Serves: 6

FUDGE CAKE

My mother-in-law always served this cake for special occasions. It's a phenomenal ending to a barbecue. The Date Cream Filling complements its rich fudge flavor.

¾ cup unsalted butter

2¼ cups granulated sugar

3 eggs

3 squares of unsweetened chocolate, melted over low heat and cooled

1½ teaspoons vanilla

3 cups flour

1½ teaspoons baking soda

¾ teaspoon salt

1½ cups ice water

Date Cream Filling (recipe follows)

1. Preheat the oven to 350° F.

2. Cream together the butter and sugar in the bowl of a mixer. Add the eggs, incorporating them one at a time into the batter, and beat until thick and fluffy. Add the cooled chocolate and the vanilla.

3. Sift together the dry ingredients and add them to the batter alternately with the ice water.

4. Grease thoroughly three 8-inch round layer pans and line the bottoms with circles of waxed paper cut to fit.

5. Divide the batter evenly among the pans and bake for 30 to 35 minutes. To test for doneness, insert a toothpick in the center of each layer. If it comes out clean and dry, the cake is done.

6. Remove the pans from the oven and let them cool on cake racks. Turn the cake out of the pans after 10 minutes' cooling time. In the meantime, make the filling.

7. Place the first cake layer on a plate and smooth on one-third of the filling.

8. Add the next layer, spread one-third of the filling over it, and top with the third layer. Spread the remaining filling over the top. This cake is best when served while still warm.

Yield: one 3-layer cake
Serves: 8

DESSERT

DATE CREAM FILLING

2 cups milk
1 cup chopped pitted dates
½ cup granulated sugar
2 tablespoons flour
2 eggs
2 teaspoons vanilla
1 cup chopped pecans, or your favorite nuts

1. Place the milk and dates in a small saucepan and warm them over low heat.

2. Meanwhile, in a small bowl combine the sugar and flour.

3. In another small bowl, beat the eggs and then add them to the sugar-flour mixture. Gradually add this mixture to the hot milk and dates.

4. Cook the filling until it thickens enough to coat a spoon, about 15 minutes. Then stir in the vanilla and nuts.

TEXAS PECAN CAKE

My Dallas buddies gave me this recipe years ago. It's perfectly outrageous served after barbecue, and, quite frankly, it's wonderful anytime you can get it!

1 pound unsalted butter
2 cups granulated sugar
6 eggs, well beaten
1 teaspoon lemon extract
4 cups unbleached flour
1½ teaspoons baking powder
4 cups pecan halves
2 cups white raisins

1. Preheat the oven to 300°F. Grease and lightly flour a 9¾-inch tube pan. Shake out any excess flour from the pan.

2. With a mixer or by hand, blend the butter and sugar together in a large bowl; beat until the mixture is light and fluffy.

3. Gradually add the eggs and lemon extract, and beat well.

4. Sift the flour and baking powder together three times; add the nuts and raisins.

5. Gradually add the dry ingredients to the creamed mixture and blend well. Pour the batter into the tube pan. Bake 1½ to 2 hours, or until a cake tester comes out clean. Cool the cake for 15 minutes, then remove it from the pan. Serve it dusted with powdered sugar, if desired.

Yield: 1 tube pan cake
Serves: 8 to 10

PIT STOPS

Barbecue gets into your blood. Once you're hooked, you will do darn near anything to keep the habit. And a large part of the fun is in discovering a great new restaurant. In my travels I have developed a "dear-to-my-heart" list of the "Pit Stops," and here are some of the best.

EAST

O'BRIEN'S PIT BBQ
1314 Gude Drive
Rockville, Maryland
(301) 340-8596

7303 Waverly Street
Bethesda, Maryland
(301) 657-3956

O'Brien's main location is just twenty-two miles outside Washington, D.C. Owner Ken O'Brien specializes in beef brisket hickory-smoked over an inside pit. He also serves pork ribs and the standard accompaniments—slaw, baked beans, potato salad, corn-on-the-cob, and chili.

TONY ROMA'S, A PLACE FOR RIBS
400 East 57th Street
New York, New York
(212) 308-0200

Tony Roma's rib houses are located in major cities in Florida, California, Texas, Tennessee, Nevada, Hawaii, and Tokyo. Most assuredly, the secret of their success lies in the fun atmosphere, the long serving hours and the great value of high-quality, fast food, cooked to order.

SMOKEY'S
230 Ninth Avenue
New York, New York
(212) 924-8181

685 Amsterdam Avenue
New York, New York
(212) 865-2900

Josh Lewin got the inspiration to start Smokey's, now one of New York's more popular barbecue restaurants, when he ate barbecue in Kentucky on a trip ten years ago. After searching in vain for a real pit barbecue restaurant in New York, he traveled through most of the southern states, researching the subject. (See mail-order section, page 91.)

BERNIE'S HOLIDAY RESTAURANT
Exit 109, New York Quickway
Rock Hill, New York
(914) 796-3333

Bernie's has gained a reputation far and wide, even though it is in a rather out-of-the-way place. The oriental kitchen is directed by Chef Moon Fat Cheung and the continental kitchen by Bernie's son, Jay Weinstein. Jay, a graduate of the Culinary Arts Institute, lays out a fine menu, but it is chef Moon Fat who prepares the ribs. They are marinated in a terrific garlicky sauce (recipe, page 49), then carefully cooked in a Chinese smoke cabinet. These ribs are fabulous.

SOUTH

THE GOLDEN RULE
200014 Sixth Avenue South
Birmingham, Alabama
(205) 324-9445

One of the best-known barbecues in Alabama, The Golden Rule, has seven or eight franchises. All the locations specialize in smoked pork and pork ribs and also serve beef and chicken. The sauce is the key to their success, along with the fact that they pit-smoke indoors with hickory wood.

THE PIG SQUEAL
Roxanna Road (one-half mile off
   Highway 280-W)
Waverly, Alabama
(205) 887-9274

The daily menu is listed on a chalkboard and features hickory-smoked barbecued pork, chicken, and ribs. Mary Ann Newman smokes the meats outside and says she's tried all cuts of pork but she prefers boneless butts served with her own ketchup-based sauce, made with a little vinegar, a little mustard, a little sugar, a little lemon juice, and lots of other ingredients.

SONNY'S PIT BARBECUE
2700 North Waldo Road
Gainesville, Florida
(904) 378-7881

Sonny Tillman originated this famous southern chain of barbecue franchises, opening his first restaurant in 1968. They serve only pork ribs, sliced beef and chicken, and use a basting sauce specifically formulated for use during cooking. A separate sauce is served at the table. Smoking over their open pits and using only black jack oak makes the barbecue at Sonny's especially tasty.

JOHNNY HARRIS
1651 East Victory Drive
Savannah, Georgia
(912) 354-7810

Johnny Harris, a wonderful old restaurant established in 1924, really specializes in smoked meat barbecue. Their sauce brews for four hours and is made with all-natural ingredients with no preservatives. (See mail-order section, page 91.)

THE SMOKY PIG
Route 14, Box 38
Bowling Green, Kentucky
(502) 781-1712

You really can taste the hickory smoke in Ned Nickerson's chopped and sliced pork cooked in an indoor pit. And the barbecue beans are the best!

LEXINGTON BARBECUE
10 Highway 29 - 70S (on parallel
   service road)
Lexington, North Carolina
(704) 249-9814

Some say Lexington, a town of 20,000 with fifteen barbecue places, is the center of the universe for the really honest-to-goodness barbecue. One of the most famous restaurants is the Lexington Barbecue, where Wayne Monk serves up pork shoulders, slowly smoked over oak or hickory for at least nine hours. They offer a hot tangy sauce at the table, and their Barbecue Coleslaw is much like the recipe on page 72. Another popular item is a barbecue salad—lettuce, tomato and your choice of dressing, topped with chopped barbecue. Hush puppies and unlimited iced tea are featured. (See mail-order section, page 91.)

PARKER'S
Highway 301 South
Wilson, North Carolina
(919) 237-0972

In 1946, timbers were floated down the Tar River to build a one-room restaurant. Today it seats 350, but Graham Parker still raises the hogs he barbecues. Whole hogs (weighing 100 pounds dressed) are pit-cooked for ten hours. Years ago they used oak, but now, with the increased price of wood, they've developed a comparable taste quality using charcoal. For saucing these scrumptious ribs they use a cider-vinegar-based mixture with crushed red pepper, black pepper, and salt.

WARD'S BARBECUE
416 East Liberty
Sumpter, South Carolina
(803) 775-2490

Thad Ward started his restaurant almost thirty years ago with an open pit. He has since changed to electric cooking methods, but his barbecue hasn't suffered. He now operates in five locations within a 120-mile radius of Sumpter. Thad's vinegary, ketchup-base sauce has been in the family for over three generations. (See mail-order section, page 91.)

MAURICE'S PIGGY PARK
Charleston Highway
West Columbia, South Carolina
(803) 796-0220

At Maurice's Piggy Park, established almost thirty years ago, they smoke the pork for eighteen hours in a closed hickory pit, seasoning the meat as it smokes. This is definitely a memorable place, combining one of the country's largest drive-ins with indoor service. They feature three sauces:

Regular: A blend of mustard, apple cider vinegar, soy sauce, peppers and other spices;

Hickory: Similar to regular, but with added hickory smoke flavoring;

Spicy Hot: With an added dash of extra-hot spices.

(See mail-order section, page 91.)

David Brown's Hickory House Pit Bar-B-Q
207 Palmetto Avenue
Winnsboro, South Carolina
(803) 635-4324

David Brown cooks his whole hogs long and slow, about twelve to fourteen hours. Then, when the meat is ready to fall from the bone, it is finely chopped and seasoned with his special vinegar-pepper, low-country sauce. David's ribs have been called the "leanest, moistest, hickory-smokiest barbecue in the area."

Charlie Vergos Rendezvous
52 South Second
Memphis, Tennessee
(901) 523-2746

Located downtown in a basement space off an alley near the Peabody Hotel, Charlie Vergos Rendezvous has a totally unique underground atmosphere. Their ribs are basted with a vinegar/water baste and then cooked over charcoal for two hours. Before serving, they're seasoned with Charlie's special blend of herbs and spices. A hot spicy barbecue sauce is served at the table.

Midwest

Carson's
612 N. Wells Street
Chicago, Illinois
(312) 280-9200

5970 North Ridge
Chicago, Illinois
(312) 271-4000

8617 Niles Center Road
Skokie, Illinois
(312) 675-6800

The ribs at Carson's, which garnered the Spectacular Slab Award from *Chicago* Magazine's Rib Report in 1979, are truly outrageous. Their baby back ribs served with cheesy scalloped potatoes, salt sticks and onion rolls, make a banquet—also available take-out.

Arthur Bryant's
1727 Brooklyn
Kansas City, Missouri
(816) 231-1123

Arthur Bryant got started way back in the dust-bowl days of the Great Depression. He loves new customers, but ignores inquiries and mail-order requests for his meats and sauces: "You can get anything at all you want from me, but ya gotta come here and get it!" Arthur Bryant's marvelously smoky ribs are a definite reason to go to Kansas City, MO.

MISSISSIPPI SALOON & BARBECUE SHACK
1315 Mississippi
St. Louis, Missouri
(314) 436-2700

What makes this barbecue special, according to Bruce Homeyer, part owner, is the fact that it is custom-smoked indoors with pecan wood. The restaurant serves barbecued ribs, specially made sausage, and sandwiches from smoked top rounds of beef and boneless hams—plus their own great, hot, tomato-base sauce.

THE GROUND FLOOR
22837 Chagrin Boulevard
Beachwood, Ohio
(216) 991-5080

The Ground Floor won first place in 1979 in the annual Cleveland "Rib Burnoff," which was no surprise because they use Canadian baby back ribs (reputed to be the most expensive and *best!*) and the chef's secret mild, sweet red sauce. They also cater your own "backyard barbecue," barbecuing anything your little heart desires on their specially made charcoal grills.

SOUTHWEST

POWDRELL'S
11309 Central, N.E.
Albuquerque, New Mexico
(505) 298-6766

At Powdrell's, ribs are cooked the authentic way—in pits, over hickory wood, maintained at a steady 250° F for ten hours. The sauce, essentially the same as the one developed by Mr. Powdrell's great-great-great-great-grandmother, simmers long and slow. (See mail-order section, page 91.)

QUARTERS
4516 Wyoming, N.E.
Albuquerque, New Mexico
(505) 299-9864

905 Yale, S.E.
Albuquerque, New Mexico
(505) 843-7505

The ribs are the big item here. Constantine Nellos, the owner, relies on a meat packer to sell him presmoked quality ribs (he assures), so he doesn't have to worry about pits, smokehouses, or wood supplies. When asked about his success, he says, "We really believe in giving high quality with good prices."

HANS BARBECUE, INC.
4101 N.W. 10th
Oklahoma City, Oklahoma
(405) 942-2473

Crispy on the outside, juicy on the inside, Hans's version of baby back ribs, hickory-smoked for hours, is my idea of perfection. Coupled with spicy hot-and-sour New Mexico sauce, they are available regular or hot. (See mail order section, page 91.)

SONNY BRYAN'S
2202 Inwood Road
Dallas, Texas
(214) 357-7120

Run by a very independent, third-generation descendent of an Irishman named Red Bryan, Sonny Bryan's is a small place with school desks for "eatin' in." Operating on a strictly cash basis, he just plain doesn't want to fool with anything other than serving outrageous barbecue.

THE CACTUS BAR-B-Q
1815½ North Main
Junction, Texas
(915) 446-2478

The Cactus Bar-B-Q is right smack in Texas hill country. Owner Jimmy Airheart cooks brisket, ribs, chicken, and wonderful German sausages over mesquite coals in his sixteen-foot outdoor pit. He uses a salt, red pepper, black pepper combination to season the meat before cooking; then has a sauce he uses to keep the meat moist while it is in the warming ovens; and another made especially for eating with your meal.

WEST

R.J.'S
252 North Beverly Drive
Beverly Hills, California
(213) 274-3474/274-7427

Owner Bob Morris claims that R.J.'s has the largest salad bar in the continental United States—a clue to his intention that his restaurant be different from the typical barbecue place. Using real hickory wood for smoking and a ketchup-based sauce, R.J.'s serves smoked chicken, smoked duck, smoked beef ribs, and smoked baby back pork ribs. They also have a catering company that Bob says is nonstop busy.

LA MONT'S
329 North El Camino Real
Encinitas, California
(714) 753-1251

El Camino North Plaza
   (Mann Theatre Complex)
2641 Vista Way #4
Oceanside, California
(714) 439-1652

The recipes featured at La Mont's authentic barbecue were created more than 100 years ago by the owner's great-grandmother, using techniques brought to America by French hunters—slowly smoking marinated meats and fish over smoldering hardwood until crispy outside and tender inside. La Mont serves barbecued chicken, pork, beef, ham, and spareribs, with all the accessories.

FLOYD & ILA'S OKLAHOMA STYLE HICKORY BAR-B-Q
5830 Telegraph Avenue
Oakland, California
(415) 653-4412

Floyd & Ila's is not an actual restaurant—it's a take-out concession run from a liquor store. Floyd uses a specially designed pit and smokes the ribs four and a half to five hours, burning hickory wood shipped from Ponca City, Oklahoma, where he spent much of his childhood. He also sells smoked and sliced top round (or sirloin) for sandwiches with his sauce on the side, and smoked chicken. (See mail-order section, page 91.)

FIREHOUSE NO. 1 BAR-B-Q
501 Clement Street
San Francisco, California
(415) 386-5882

Owner Carl English's original barbecue inspirations can be traced to his childhood in Leavenworth, Kansas, where his grandfather sold barbecued ribs from a pushcart and his mother and grandmother made the sauce. His restaurant offers barbecued ribs, chicken and smoky links cooked slowly over hardwood coals. And the sauce, seasoned to perfection, comes in three varieties:
One Alarm: For a light touch, mild;
Two Alarm: Watch out, hot;
Three Alarm: Where's the nearest fireman?
(See mail-order section, page 91.)

HOG HEAVEN
770 Stanyan Street
San Francisco, California
(415) 668-2038

Originally from Memphis, Tennessee, Andrea Martin, Bay Area resident and lawyer for ten years, missed her native barbecue so much that she decided to bring it to San Francisco. She serves pork shoulder which is cooked for eight to ten hours over mesquite

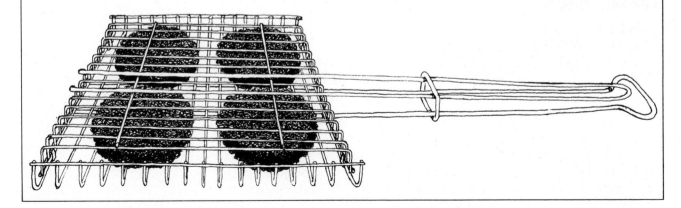

and hickory coals in a huge brick oven "pit," then pulled and brushed with a "sweet, tangy, spicy-but-not-too-hot taste of Memphis." Hog Heaven also serves barbecued sausage, chicken and ribs.

SMOKIN' WILLIE'S
603 Main Street
Frisco, Colorado
(303) 668-3906

Bill Dickson's barbecue technique is open-pit. He cooks "out back" and gets his wood from a man who clears orchards, using predominantly apple and peach to give his barbecue a sweeter-than-usual taste. The sauce is Alabama-inspired—his uncle's secret recipe.

SCRUBBY'S SMOKEHOUSE RESTAURANT
8775 Fairview Avenue
Boise, Idaho
(208) 375-8474

Ab Road, "1 mile from the end of the world"
Mountain Home, Idaho
(208) 832-7074

Owner Jim Birchfield claims to have the only genuine Texas smokehouse in Idaho. He smokes his brisket, pork and beef ribs, fresh leg of pork, ham, turkey and chicken with apple wood and cooks his beans in a giant above-ground pit.

M & S MEATS
Rollins, Montana
(406) 844-3414

Milton and Sylvia Oberg have owned this meat shop located near the entrance to Glacier National Park for over five years. They barbecue roasts and ribs in their outdoor pit. (See mail-order section, page 91.)

J-K WILD BOAR SOUL BARBECUE PIT
2506 Cherry Street
Seattle, Washington
(206) 329-4204

THE BOAR'S NEST
1133 23rd Avenue
Seattle, Washington
(206) 322-6430

James Beal has Seattle's Texas-style barbecue market covered forever with these gems. He pit-smokes beef brisket, ribs (pork and beef), chickens, and sausage over alder wood. Both restaurants serve two sauces: regular is hot, and hot is phenomenal. (See recipe, page 22.)

SWEET'S CAFE
Star Route #2 West
Rock Springs, Wyoming
(307) 362-3125

Edna Sweet's been in this business for thirty-one years and seems to have loved every minute of it! She barbecues the pork ribs, beef, and chicken outside over oak coals and serves them with her own special homemade sauce.

MAIL-ORDER BARBECUE

If you don't want to make your own sauce, I've rounded up a wide assortment of mail-order sources for you. All are known in their locales (some nationally) for having the finest quality products. Write for a price list and then send a check to cover the cost of the product plus postage and handling.

EAST

★ RICHARD S. KUTAS COMPANY
177 Military Road
Buffalo, NY 14027
For homemade liquid smoke and smoke-house information.

★ JANE BUTEL'S PECOS VALLEY SPICE CO. TEXAS BARBECUE SAUCE
45-39 37th Street
Long Island City, NY 11101
A thick, smoky, somewhat spicy Texas-style barbecue sauce.

★ LIFESPICE
60 West 15th Street
New York, NY 10011
A vinegary, salt-free barbecue sauce spiced with pure ground red chili.

★ SMOKEY'S
230 Ninth Avenue
New York, NY 10001
A ketchup-base in three heats:
Mild: Tangy and flavorful
Medium: Pretty good bite
Hot: Hot!

SOUTH

★ JOHNNY HARRIS SAUCE CO.
2801 Wicklow Street
Savannah, GA 31404
A mustard-vinegar-ketchup-base southern sauce.

★ LEXINGTON BARBECUE
10 Highway 79-70S
Lexington, NC 27292
A peppery mix of ketchup and spices in a vinegar base. This thinner, basting-type sauce is great for all outdoor barbecues.

★ WARD'S BARBECUE SAUCE CO.
617 Boulevard Road
Sumpter, SC 29150
A ketchup- and vinegar-base sauce Southern-style.

★ **MAURICE'S PIGGY PARK**
P.O. Box 847
W. Columbia, SC 29169
A traditional mustard-vinegar-base sauce,
plus two variations—hickory and spicy hot.

MIDWEST

★ **CURLEY'S FAMOUS HICKORY BURGERS, INC.**
2400 Line Road, P.O. Box 1584
Hutchinson, KS 67501
A smoky, all-natural ketchup-base sauce.

SOUTHWEST

★ **HANS BARBECUE INC.**
4101 N.W. 10th Street
Oklahoma City, OK 73107
(405) 942-2473
A tangy, tart sauce in hot or mild strength.

★ **SANTA CRUZ CHILI & SPICE COMPANY**
Box 177
Tumacacori, AZ 85640
A chili-spiced, all-purpose barbecue sauce.

★ **POWDRELL'S**
11309 Central, N.E.
Albuquerque, NM 87123
A somewhat spicy, ketchup-base sauce.

WEST

★ **HOWARD'S FAMOUS TEXAS BARBECUE CO.**
9228 South Western Avenue #1
Los Angeles, CA 90047

Western style: All-purpose, sweet, smoky,
    mildly spicy
Southern style: Spicy-sweet molasses flavor,
    good with pork and poultry
Texas style: Sweet, smoky, *hot* and spicy;
    good with beef or pork.

★ **FIREHOUSE #1**
501 Clement Street
San Francisco, CA 94118
A ketchup-base sauce from a family recipe,
available in three strengths.

★ **FLOYD & ILA'S OKLAHOMA STYLE HICKORY BAR-B-Q**
5830 Telegraph Avenue
Oakland, CA 94609
A spicy ketchup-base sauce.

★ **M & S MEATS**
Rollins, MT 59931
A tomato-base sauce with vinegar and
spices.

INDEX